The Women's Money® Guide to Budgeting, Spending & Saving Money

Gina Robison-Billups and

Women's Money® Expert Contributors

Table of Contents

About Women's Money®

The Women's Money Council, a national council of community, financial industry, and policy leaders, conducts research and provides women programs for advocacy, education, and mentorship in order to foster financial independence, social and economic justice.

84% of women say they are not understanding or receiving information from financial and investment institutions. Currently, 1 in 3 women lives in or on the brink of poverty. 90% of women say they are completely or mostly unprepared for retirement. As a result, 3 out of 5 women in the U.S. will retire in poverty. Why is that?

Most financial experts believe that college savings and retirement planning are put off because women say, "Oh, I have time to figure that out later" - then years have gone by and they've run out of time. We don't believe that is true. We believe that this procrastination mindset is a small part of a bigger picture. It is not the cause. It is the effect.

Women's Money® has developed a unique proprietary system to close the three gaps women experience in understanding and managing money concepts.

Clearly there is a communication gap – a big one, and reducing the Communication Gap is the first space in which Women's Money® sets out to make a difference. We are developing the tools and methods to reduce that gap. However, it's more than just a Communication Gap. There's also a Confidence Gap and Action Gap. The old adage, "you'd do better if you knew better" doesn't hold true when fear, confusion or insecurity are involved. Women's Money® is developing and implementing methods that reduce the gaps in Communication, Confidence and Action and support women into taking achieving measurable results in their path to financial wellness.

Women's Money® has been able to successfully pilot its unique and innovative financial education program in Nevada and has now expanded to several locations nationwide. Program ONE, the foundation building phase of the process includes mentoring events, personal mentoring, and conferences.

2/3rds
of American household breadwinners and co-breadwinners are women.
(The Shriver Report)

90%
of women are mostly or completely unprepared for retirement.
(Sheconomy)

3 of 5
Women age 65 and older (married and single) cannot pay for their basic daily expenses.
(Wowonline.org)

1 out of 3
women live in poverty or on the brink of poverty.
(The Shriver Report)

84%
feel misunderstood by investment and financial companies.
(Sheconomy)

Women's Money®
Program ONE

The Women's Money® Program One is designed to help women have a place of support while they take action on their personal finances to create a strong foundation. "One" is the first phase of the Women's Money® program. It's a nice idea to think about growing your money, but if you are drowning in debt or don't have a safety-net established, then growing your money may be a risk you cannot yet take. Building a strong foundation is the first step to building a brighter.

Program ONE focuses on three core concepts to build a strong foundation:

- Financial Management (Budgeting/ Debt/ Spending/ Money Triggers / Goals and Organization)
- Financial Safeguards (Savings/ Income Development/ Credit/ Identity Theft)
- Financial Protection (Insurance/ Taxes/ Retirement / Investing)

What you get when you join One:

- The Women's Money® Guidebook.
- Your own Personal Women's Money® Mentor.
- Your own online Mentoring Portal.
- Advanced Access to Conference Tickets & Scholarships.
- LIFETIME membership! You can attend any Program ONE mentoring event for free. (see details)
- Mentoring support systems.
- Exclusive Invitations to Mentoring Events.

Programs similar to just one part of the Women's Money system would easily cost you $297 to $1789 a year.

Women's Money is a non-profit organization; therefore, Program ONE is free to you.

About Women's Money®
Program TWO

Some of the women in Program ONE are ready for us to launch the next level with Program TWO and attend the Women's Money® Wealth Building Bootcamp. After women have created a strong financial foundation in Program One, they can apply to join Program Two. A mentor must have a personal review of the mentee's financial foundation, and give a recommendation as to their readiness to join Program Two.

What makes Program TWO so exciting is that women can be ready for Program TWO after only 6-18 months in Program ONE. When you realize that some of these women haven't been able to get to this point with existing resources in the last 20-40 years, this makes their achievement even more outstanding and exciting.

Current Women's Money® Two Program Components:

- Women's Money® Wealth Building Bootcamp
- Women's Money® Wealth Building and Investing Circles

To be in Women's Money® Two, you need to participate in Women's Money® One. Let your mentor know that you are setting a goal to participate in Two. Your mentor will work with you to make sure you are ready to receive your invitation to the Women's Money® Wealth Building Bootcamp.

At the Women's Money® Wealth Building Bootcamp you will experience:

- Understanding Investment Terms.
- Understanding Investment Basics.
- Determining How Much You Need for Retirement.
- How to Buy Investments.
- How to Read a Financial Statement...
  and much, much more.

Our Contributors are
Your Board of Advisors

Our dear friend and advocate, Gail Perry-Mason, advises us to create a personal financial "Board of Directors" who can help advise each of us to our personal financial goals and freedom. Please consider our contributors of this book as your virtual Board of Directors to help you make healthy personal financial choices.

Thank you to all the these wonderful experts who made this book possible.

Women's Money® Founder and Creator, Gina Robison-Billups

Gina Robison-Billups, serves as president of The International Association of Working Mothers (tiawm), a charitable, tax-exempt, 501(c)(3) organization dedicated to making a significant difference in building and sustaining healthy communities by unlocking the potential of working mothers through advocacy and education.

Ms. Robison-Billups founded Women's Money® - a unique, proprietary financial education, support and accomplishment system for women, girls and families. The program was piloted in Nevada with two conferences in June 2012 and support system. Since the launch, Women's Money® has hosted seven conference, expanded into Spanish, brought financial education to over 4000 Nevadans, and has grown nationwide delivering over 30,000 hours of financial education to people nationwide.

Robison-Billups is the founder and past-president of the National Association For Moms In Business representing the interests of more than 15 million entrepreneurial and executive mothers. Under her leadership the organization grew to ten locations nationwide, published Moms In Business Magazine, and produced several events including the Nevada Women's Leadership Summit - the annual event celebrating the achievements of Nevada's Women and identifying high-growth opportunities in our state. During her tenure, Robison-Billups created the first national Crowdfunded Business Grant which generated almost $25,000 for micro-business Moms In Business Grant finalists. She is a recognized leader in microbusiness and microfinance issues. After the organization marked its 10th Anniversary, Robison-Billups' officially resigned from service to dedicate more time to Women's Money®. Moms In Business has since been acquired by a new leadership organization.

Recognitions

Her work with home based business owners and mom business owners has earned her the title of the Home Based Business Advocate for the state of Nevada in 2003 and 2007 from the Small Business Administration, and she was named as a national finalist for The Women's Congress 2008 Champion for Women Awards, and a finalist for the ATHENA Leadership Award from the Nevada Women's Chamber of Commerce. Robison-Billups has been named one of Vegas Inc.'s Women to Watch for 2012 because of these conferences and the unique and results-driven programming of the Women's Money® Council.

Appointments

Robison-Billups is the first Nevada woman appointed as a member to the National Women's Business Council (NWBC.gov), a nonpartisan federal advisory council created to serve as an independent source of advice and policy recommendations to the President, Congress, and the U.S. Small Business Administration on economic issues of importance to women business owners. For the first time, moms in business and micro-business owners had a seat at the table to advise the President, Congress, and the SBA via Gina's service to the Council. Robison-Billups has previously served as the Co-Chair of the National Healthcare Committee for Women Impacting Public Policy (WIPP). She currently serves as WIPP's Nevada Instant Impact Leader and is a member of the Advisory Council for the Alliance for Nevada Non-Profits (ANN).

Books & Publications

- The Accomplishment Series
- Marketing 2 Moms: How to Capture the Attention, Interest and Sales of America's #1 Consumer
- Why 5% Succeed: The 5 Principles of Predictable Profit
- The Women's Money® Guide to Budgeting, Spending & Saving Money.

Mikelann Valterra

Mikelann is an author, speaker and leader in the field of personal finance. She has been a money coach/ Financial Recovery Coach, working with professionals for over 15 years. Mikelann addresses practical money matters as well as the emotional components that often fuel unhealthy financial behaviors. Her passion is to help professionals escape the money fog, feel more in control of their finances and love their financial life. She believes everyone can truly heal their relationship to money.

In 2011 Mikelann co-founded the MoneyMinder company- www.moneyminderonline.com- with Karen McCall. MoneyMinder offers subscription based spending plan software designed to help people gain control of their finances and experience flexible, guilt-free spending.

Mikelann is also on the faculty of the Financial Recovery Institute, founded by Karen McCall, where she helps train new money coaches.

She is the author of Why Women Earn Less: How to make what you're really worth, as well as multiple workbooks and audios. Mikelann has appeared on dozens of radio shows, television spots and in newspapers across the United States, as well as blogging for Forbes.

Born and raised in the northwest, Mikelann first studied economics and then earned a masters in Conscious Studies and Psychology. She capped it off with her certification as a Financial Recovery Counselor and Coach. After almost two decades of working with people on their relationship to money, Mikelann brings a deep understanding of psychology and human potential to the fields of personal finance, consumer debt issues and the emotional language of money.

Gerri Detweiler

Helping consumers find reliable answers to their credit questions has been the theme of Gerri Detweiler's work for the past twenty years.

As an expert on consumer credit issues, she has been interviewed for more than 3000 news interviews including The Today Show, Dateline NBC,The New York Times, USA Today and Reader's Digest. She has also testified before Congress.

As a speaker, she has addressed both consumer and industry audiences nationwide. She was a featured speaker in an 18-city speaking tour and has been a repeat guest at several events for financial planners.

As an educator, she is the author or co-author of five books:

- Reduce Debt, Reduce Stress (Good Advice Press 2009)
- Debt Collection Answers: How to Use Debt Collection Laws to Protect Your Rights (2009)
- The Ultimate Credit Handbook (Plume, 1993, revised 2003), which was featured in Money magazine as one of the five best new personal finance books of the year when released.
- Invest In Yourself: Six Secrets to a Rich Life (Wiley, October 1998)
- Slash Your Debt: Save Money & Secure Your Future (Financial Literacy Center, 1999).

Gerri is Director of Consumer Education for Credit.com, one of the web's leading personal finance websites. Many of her articles also appear on partner websites, including MSN Money and ABCNews.com.

She is the host of a live weekly radio program Talk Credit Radio. Podcasts of many of the episodes are available online.

Gerri reaches thousands of consumers each month through these websites, as well as numerous others for which she contributes content. She also hosted a weekly financial radio show and several hundred of her interviews are still available at that site for consumers to listen to online.

Gerri holds a B.A. in International Business/Political Affairs from Taylor University, and an M.A. in Adult Education/ Psychology from Vermont College.

Carrie Rocha

I am Carrie Rocha. After my husband and I paid off $50,000+ in debt I felt compelled to share what we'd learned with others. Pocket Your Dollars is the place where I share.

We Got Out of Debt

Our journey started in June 2006 when my husband and I made a commitment. We decided to get out of debt and to stay out debt for the rest of our lives. Much like a new mom who panics when she realizes that the teeny baby is her responsibility, I felt afraid and overwhelmed by our decision, but we didn't back down.

We were and are middle class folks that had student loan debt, a car loan, tax debt, and more. We recognized the need to have discretionary income to pay off the existing debt and save for future purchases. Two ways we could do it - increase our income or decrease expense. We opted to start by decreasing our expense. I mean, who wants to work more hours in the day if they don't have to?

Marco and I split our household expenses between us. Each was charged to reduce expense in any creative way possible so that we could start building an emergency fund, saving for expected non-routine things and paying down our debt.

It was November 2009 when I wrote the check that paid off the last of those $50,000 in debts. In 2.5 years we'd done what seemed impossible at the start. Today, we still have our first mortgage, but are paying it down.

The Seeds that Started Pocket Your Dollars

When we got out of debt it was the start of the Great Recession. People I love were losing their homes and their jobs at the same time we were experiencing more financial stability than we ever had. I felt compelled to act.

I had a seed of a desire in me. I wanted to teach a small group of women at my local church about the things I'd learned related to grocery coupons. That was my ultimate goal at the time.

In late February 2009 I received disappointing news at work. I had been passed over for a promotion to be the President of my company. The Board opted for an outsider with a stronger marketing background. Unfortunately, the organization could no longer afford a COO and I would eventually be laid off.

We were scared because just a few weeks prior to receiving that news, Marco had quit his long-time job as an International Sales Manager to become a stay-at-home dad by day and a grad school student by night. I was the sole breadwinner and had just learned that after the new President was acclimated into his role, I'd be unemployed.

The day after hearing about the impending layoff I was invited to teach a money-saving class to stay-at-homes. I jumped at the opportunity because it would give me something and someone else to focus on while I processed my own disappointment.

While I taught that very first class I said out loud, "This would be so much easier if I had a website." Two weeks went by and I could not shake the feeling that I had to start a website.

It was a crazy prospect at the time. I was still working full-time as Chief Operating Officer (it was 9 months until I was laid off). We had a 3-month old baby and 2-year old toddler. My husband was in graduate school at night. Nonetheless, I stepped out.

Pocket Your Dollars is Born - I started this website on March 16, 2009 with this blog post. My heart's desire was to provide a community service to a few dozen women I personally knew. I had no idea what was in store for me or for this website.

Ten days after the site launched, my local FOX affiliate did a story about me and the site. Then I spoke with a reporter from the

Minneapolis Star Tribune. Then a local cable station wanted to interview me. Then one thing led to another and by the time the first year had gone by I'd done almost 100 media appearances. I became the go-to consumer and money-saving expert in the Minneapolis area.

After I'd been doing this for 6 months I was receiving invitations from companies like General Mills. They wanted me to teach their employees how to stretch their paychecks as part of their wellness program. At the same time I started getting national recognition in outlets like Yahoo! Finance and Wall Street Journal Radio. With so much going on I scaled back to part-time at my day job, in September 2009, to devote even more to this website.

Finally, in January 2010 I was laid off from that Minneapolis-based non-profit. That was 10 months after Pocket Your Dollars' launch. Marco and I decided to take a calculated risk into self-employment and devote even more to it. We have not looked back.

Now we steward a community of more 1.3 million unique visitors annually. I continue to do public speaking, make media appearances and am author my first book Pocket Your Dollars: 5 Attitude Changes That Will Help You Pay Down Debt, Avoid Financial Stress, and Keep More of What You Make available from Amazon or BN.com (Bethany House). I also serve on the National Women's Money Council, the Advisory Board for Affiliate Summit, am Consumer Editor at Wisebread.com, am serve on the Performance Marketing Association's Publisher Recruitment Council.

I am speechless and humbled at this incredible path I've walked so far.

Leisa Peterson

My name is Leisa Peterson and I am a strategic wealth coach and founder of WealthClinic, a community for learning, sharing and mindfully expanding our experiences with money and wealth building. I am really glad you are here!

Part of our mission includes sharing the importance of having greater mindfulness in all that we do.

Mindfulness is our innate ability to be present, as well as composed, and to pause before we react to the challenges of our busy lives. As opposed to mindlessness, a mindful person pays greater attention to and has more control over their actions of body, speech and mind which helps them to become a better leader, partner, friend and co-worker.

Our history begins with the convergence of two diametrically opposed worlds: spirituality and finance.

At first glance, nearly everyone thinks these two worlds are complete opposites. Because at best, spirituality is grounded in love and compassion. And at its worst, finance is fueled by greed. But what I eventually discovered is these two worlds are direct reflections of each other.

To understand how, let's rewind a bit...Back in 1999, I was enjoying a successful career in the financial world. That same year, a family tragedy occurred. To help me heal, I started studying spiritual philosophy and trying to meditate. That's when I began straddling the two worlds.

As soon as I began looking introspectively, I felt pulled to learn and practice more. At first I attended retreats, signing up for longer ones each time. Eventually, I taught others how to meditate and use mindfulness in their day-to-day lives.

During that time, I was also working for a large bank. While at the bank, I watched and participated in the euphoric economic rise of the mind-2000's. Followed by the fiscal meltdown of 2007-2008 and the painful aftermath of the Great Recession.

This front row seat to mayhem caused me to ask many questions like:

- Why do we repeatedly engage with money in very unconscious ways?
- Why does money, at times, make me and other people do stupid and silly things?
- Is there a way to stop this behavior by applying mindfulness to money?

Since I couldn't find anyone to answer these questions (from either world), I decided to figure them out on my own.

I've always loved research, so I dove deeply into researching the answers. But with each psychological study, expert interview, or book I read...my questions grew. After years of study, I ended up with more questions, but no concrete answers.

Eventually, in my position as a financial adviser, I started asking my clients about their personal experiences with money. That's when the pieces of the puzzle really came together. I combined their feedback with principles from psychology, sociology, biology/neurology, and philosophy. Then added my 22 years of working with money. And my 15 years of personal spiritual development.

It took all of this to create the comprehensive system we apply at WealthClinic. People using the system see quick, dramatic and positive changes in their experiences with money and much more.

I believe the fact it took insight from so many fields reflects the complexity of money in our modern lives. It's no wonder we keep repeating our limiting and damaging money behaviors, no matter how hard we try to change!

After watching so many people use our process, here's what really blew my mind...When we change our experiences with money and learn how to see it with a new lens, we throw a new door wide open. A door to life fulfillment (and greater prosperity!) that often remains undiscovered and closed. But when you open that door, life changes in bigger and better ways than we can ever imagine.

Unlike other wealth building programs that merely tell you to change your money mindset and then everything will improve, WealthClinic programs teach you exactly HOW to:

- #1. Improve your inner game, change your money mindset, and take your wealth building habits to the next level,
- #2. Own your whole story so that you become the creator of the life you want to live,
- #3. Create a money mind map for where you want to go, why you want to go there and how you are going to get there, and
- #4. Implement your strategy using a broad range of tools and mental exercises that support your success in a way that fits perfectly for YOU!

Namaste,
Leisa Peterson, MBA, CFP®
Founder, WealthClinic

Brenda Prinzavalli

Brenda Prinzavalli shares her passion for life through sharing her passion for applying organizational philosophies to all areas of your personal and professional life.

Even though her ability to communicate organizing strategies has been with her from the start, in 2003 she made it her official business. Brenda founded Balanced Organizing Solutions, LLC, a professional organizing service, to assist businesses and individuals in finding solutions for their busy lives. She offers on-site and virtual consulting, as well as hands-on organizing services. She delivers upbeat and interactive training programs, corporate workshops and seminars that encourage audiences to transform their lives through mastery of behaviors that lead to control of their actions and environment.

Brenda works with others in a variety of ways:
As a professional organizer, trainer and consultant... Brenda regularly consults with businesses and corporations to implement more profitable work strategies and achieve greater work/life balance through streamlined systems. She also works with individuals and families who want to simply their lives to gain more control over daily activities and create more time to pursue their passions.

As an author and speaker...she draws upon the wisdom of her experiences as a trainer, consultant and educator. Brenda is the author of several organizing books—all of which are essential reading for being more organized, more effective and creating results.

Brenda's Philosophy:

"When you know where you want to go, it doesn't matter where you are. The focus is on the path ahead and how to get there using organization as the guidepost."

People make statements about their current state of organization and apologize; they say they are embarrassed or are in such overwhelm it paralyzes them. You get to leave all of that behind when we create a plan because the more you focus on your current dissatisfaction, the longer you will stay there. Look up, look ahead and start moving!

"Getting and being organized is not about being rigid and boring, it is about being flexible and creative."

Creating organizational solutions is one of the most creative processes around. There are so many components to take into consideration before an ideal solution is crafted. Learning styles, personality styles, strengths, weaknesses, self-discipline, available time, resources, tools, key individuals, support and overall commitment to the outcome all play a piece in crafting the best solution. Each piece is part of the puzzle that ends up being your picture.

Kat Bellucci

Kat Bellucci, Your Money Gal™ , and Host of Women's Money® Radio has dedicated her life to providing solutions in all aspects of her career. From early on, she always asked the questions that others wanted answers to. She believes that knowledge is the power to making better decisions.

With more than 25 years of professional experience, Kat Bellucci specializes in helping businesses grow and prosper through Advanced Planning Strategies.

Kat lives her life by a couple of rules:

"You can make a difference in someone's life every day" and "If you always give, you will always have".

Kat attributes her success to the "old school" honesty and integrity that her parents instilled in her. She educates business owners and individuals how to evaluate their individual needs which will allow them to identify the areas that require strategies and solutions. Kat believes that you can't create "your wealth" with someone else's plan. She also believes that everyone is entitled to the best someone has to give. That said, she works utilizing the "Collaborative Team Approach". Allowing a team of experts in the various areas that impact your wealth -- great minds coming together offering improved strategic solutions. The result; the individual or business receives is more efficient information enabling them to make better decisions.

Kat's goal is to really make a difference in the lives of those around her. It is her passion for knowledge and ability to teach others what is available to them that made her a perfect fit to become the host of the Women's Money® Radio Show. As the show's host, Kat interviews experts in all the areas that impact a person's wealth such as financial investments, retirement, insurance, budgeting, tax, structure, wealth transfer, estate planning and business continuation needs. Seeking experts who can enhance a woman's ability to make better financial decisions, Kat's role is to help empower women with their "mind, wallet and soul" to achieve their personal financial goals.

Nobody should be intimidated by their money or making financial decisions, they should make their financial decisions with confidence. Kat brings a friendly, supportive voice to the money conversation.

Kat has achieved top honors throughout her professional career and always stays on top of her industry trends, rulings, news and products with constant research, commitment to detail and diligence. Kat is writing Your Money Gal's™ Guidebook to share all the critical information she has accumulated with her listeners to use. Kat has served on the boards and/or been a member of NAIFA, NAFMIB Las Vegas, Clark County Bar Association, AGC, WIC, AICPA, SNEPC, ASPAA and was the co-host of Mom's Making a Million radio show.

Kat's work and life motto: "Treat everyone the way you want to be treated, and you will always be successful in life", Because You Can Make A Difference In Someone's Life Everday!

Kat is the mother of two teenagers and six dogs and cats.

Elaine Starling

Elaine Starling is the President and Chief Innovation Officer for Starling Media Services, Inc. a boutique marketing firm helping purpose-driven women entrepreneurs become legacy leaders; women who communicate effectively with engaging ease to make a lasting difference in the world, increase their profits and enjoy highly-successful and fulfilling businesses. Elaine is an acknowledged thought leader and marketing master, generating over $100 million for her clients by creating innovative programs that increase participation, process improvement, positioning and profit.

Elaine is the author of "Why 5% Succeed: The 5 Principles of Predictable Profit" and the host of the "Why 5% Succeed" show and podcast. Elaine's new book, "How to Give Yourself a Raise" is also garnering rave reviews.

In addition to her work with the Women's Money® Council, Elaine has been the emcee of the Women's Money® Conference for two years. Elaine also serves on the Board of Directors for Women Impacting Public Policy, a bi-partisan organization representing 70 professional women's organizations and over 8.3 million women business owners. Elaine is also a member of the Advisory Board for Enterprising Women, an organization supporting over 300,000 women entrepreneurs around the world.

As a sought-after speaker, consultant, columnist, mentor, and a very successful entrepreneur, Elaine enjoys teaching her unique Why 5% Succeed Formula™ to women worldwide. Elaine's national and international clients include WebEx, Shutterfly, Symantec, Sprint, Mattel Toys, Orion Pictures, and many others.

Julie Macc

Julie Macc, certified Credit/Identity Theft Specialist and author is a recognized expert on credit reporting for both consumer and business credit scoring. With more than 20 years of experience in the field, Julie is a trusted and acclaimed expert on credit reporting for both consumer and business credit scoring.

Julie serves as an expert witness/legal consultant for law firms practicing consumer credit law in both federal and state court. She has been retained as an expert witness for more than 200 consumer credit litigation cases involving lenders, banks, collection agencies, each of the three major credit bureaus, and third-party credit furnishers.

Julie has developed and led hundreds of credit score training seminars/courses for mortgage, banking and real estate professionals, as well as for general consumer audiences. She delivers keynote speeches at mortgage and real estate industry meetings for continued education training to educate and update legal and mortgage industry professionals on the current laws and reporting trends.

Budgeting Your Money

Budgeting: Strategies & Concepts

How to Prepare a Realistic Budget
Excerpt from the Women's Money® Guidebook

Many people cringe at the very idea of preparing a budget. It could be that they have a negative reaction to the word. The word budget comes from the French word for wallet, a place to keep money. Other terms used in place of "budget" include "spending plan" and "cash flow plan."

A budget is a self-made tool for directing and controlling our money. Every successful business in America uses a budget to guide operations. Every household should, too, so that families meet their important goals, cover all their expenses, live within their means, and experience the satisfaction that comes from having their finances under control.

A budget is a plan for how you will use your money. Some people shy away from preparing a written budget. They think that having a mental budget is sufficient. They also think that developing a budget is too time-consuming or involved, so they back off. Let's look at a simple, six-step process for budgeting. You should be able to prepare a monthly budget on one page! A handheld calculator will speed the process along.

Building a Realistic Budget

Step 1. Estimate your income. First determine what time period your plan will cover. The planning period may be a month, a year, or any length of time you choose. We will focus on a monthly budget. In figuring income from your earnings, include only your take-home pay or net income. This is different from your gross earnings. Your net income is what you have left after income taxes, Social Security, Medicare, insurance (health, life, disability, etc.), flexible spending plan contributions, retirement savings, and other deductions. Net income is what you have left to spend. You may have other sources of monthly income, too, such as: spouse's earnings, income from self-employment or a second job, interest or dividend income, or child support payments.

Whether you are paid weekly or every two weeks, your monthly income will need to be calculated from the actual amount of your take-home pay, regardless of how frequently you are paid.

Step 2. Estimate your expenses. People who have not tracked their spending find that estimating their expenses is the most difficult aspect of setting up a budget. You've tracked your spending for two to three months. Tracking your spending gave you a fairly good idea of how you spend your money. If you completed a Statement of Income and Expense for the previous year, you also have an additional source of information to use in estimating your future monthly expenses. You may need to consult your records, such as your check register and your receipts, for more details. Expenses may be classified as either fixed expenses or flexible expenses. Fixed expenses, like rent or mortgage payments and loan repayments, are the same each month, while flexible expenses differ each month. Common flexible expense categories are listed in the table, My Monthly Budget Estimates. They are flexible because they vary in amount, such as food; or they are "discretionary," that is, what you spend for them is at your discretion, in contrast to fixed expenses that must be paid and are usually the same amount each month.

You should consider your special financial goals to be fixed expenses. When you do this, you are more likely to fund your future financial goals. This is the idea behind the concept "pay yourself first." The table, My Monthly Budget Estimates, is a tool to help you estimate your expenses and balance your income and expenses.

Step 3. *Make adjustments to balance your budget. In a perfect world, your budget would balance perfectly on the first try. But this is the real world; so don't worry if your outgo exceeds your income on the first go-around.* See how you can bring it into balance.

Is it realistic for you to increase your income? How? Get another job? Get a raise? Hold a garage sale? Check to see if you are over-withholding your federal income taxes and, if so, you may be able to increase your take-home pay by adjusting your exemptions. Or, are you eligible for the Earned Income Tax Credit (EITC) that could increase your monthly take-home pay? The Earned Income Tax Credit is a refundable federal income tax credit for low to moderate income working individuals and families. Information on the EITC can be found on the Internal Revenue Service website at http://www.irs.gov/individuals/article/O,.id=96406,00.html

If you cannot increase your income, your other choice is to reduce your expenses to bring your budget into balance. Check over each expense category. Are you sure that you are getting the most for your money? Or are you over-paying for things that you could obtain for less? For example: 1) are you sure that your cell phone plan is the best one for the money, or could you find a better plan for less money, or 2) are you paying for a communications package that offers more Internet, cable, and telephone and texting features than you really need or use?

Make the necessary changes to your budget to bring it into balance so that your expenses do not exceed your income. Unless you balance your budget, you will be tempted to use your credit card to finance the difference.

Step 4. Try living within your budget. Until you try to live by your budget, that is, "living within your means," you have no real idea whether it works for you or not. Right now, it is only a tool on paper. Living within your budget is the main challenge of modern living! During this test period, track your spending so that you can compare actual spending to what you had budgeted. Recordkeeping during this phase is vitally important. If you cannot or do not compare what you spent (reality) with what you budgeted (what you thought you would spend), there is no point in budgeting whatsoever. Women like you with important life goals will see the budgeting process as a critical tool for achieving financial success. Getting control of money through effective budgeting is a critically important step in overall financial planning. Live within your budget for a month or two to see if it works.

Step 5. Develop and use a financial recordkeeping system that works for you. The other critical tool in the budgeting process is recordkeeping. You won't know if your budget works until you analyze your real-life spending. In Chapter 2, Money Math, you learned how to create a written record (notebook tool) to track your spending. You can continue with this method if it works for you. Summarize your monthly expenses, and compare them to what you budgeted for each expense category you established. There are many ways to keep financial records, but they all require you to summarize your monthly expenses so you can draw conclusions from the experience and know whether your budget really worked for you during your trial period.

The receipt method is a simple method for tracking spending. Just make sure you obtain a receipt for every transaction you make, whether it is made by cash, debit card, credit card, or check. Mark each receipt with the name of the budget expense category. Each week or at the end of the month, sort your receipts by budget category; tally up the results, and enter the information on a chart. By entering the summaries on a monthly basis, you will immediately see your spending trends and can easily see the times when expenses increase.

The checkbook method works well for people who make most transactions by check or debit card. The checkbook register is the primary data-entry tool. Code each transaction for the budget expense category to which it belong. Each week or at the end of the month, tally up the results by budget category. If you bank on-line, you can access your account readily. You may be able to assign a spending category to each transaction in your on-line account and then download your account information to a spreadsheet or even transmit it to another web-based financial recordkeeping system.

Record book methods work well for people who like to manually record all of their financial transactions on a daily or weekly basis. Many types of household record books are sold commercially at office supply stores, but their income and expense categories may or may not match the categories you use. You can also make your own record book by duplicating the form on the next page, My Monthly Income and Expense Record. Just label the top row with the names of your income and expense categories. At month's end, add the totals for each category. Reserve one page to use as an annual summary. At the end of the year, you will have a complete summary of income and expense. Then you can easily construct a new Statement of Income and Expense.

Computerized financial recordkeeping systems are both useful and popular. People who use these systems are able to tailor their income and expense categories to meet their needs and can effortlessly produce summary reports. Some people prefer the commercial software packages; others who know how to use electronic spreadsheets create their own financial recordkeeping systems. And others keep their financial information at special financial recordkeeping websites. The latest innovations involve web-based systems that bring together all of your financial transactions and allow access by computer, cell phone, or personal digital assistants (PDAs).

Step 6. Adjust your budget to reflect your real life experiences with it. After following your budget for a couple of months, you should be in a position to know if it works for you. Fine-tune your budget categories, and reallocate your income to meet your needs. **A budget is a very flexible tool if you will make the necessary adjustments. A budget is not a strait jacket. If it doesn't work, fix it; don't abandon it!**

Saving 40% of Your Income?

There is a growing movement amongst personal finance "gurus" to try to live on 60% of what you earn.   That may seem impossible right now, but many people are working towards that goal. It's not easy, and it's not fast, but it can be very rewarding. So how do you get to the point to save 40% of your income? Budgeting is the key.
1.   Make a goal you can feel committed to. If you cannot start with 40%, try 10 or 20%.
2.   Know that there are going to be months you miss your goal, so be sure to just save something…anything. Let go of the disappointment and start again.
3.   Do your budget (again, and again…most of us forget things the first go around).
4.   Adjust your spending habits to save money.
5.   Negotiate or change essential services to save money.
6.   Calculate: If you adjusted your spending habits and paid off debt, how much would you be able to save?   20%, 30%, 40%?
7.   Pay off your debt - add the money you have saved by adjusting spending and bills to your payments.

8. Adjust your mindset to feel as if you only make 60% of your actual paycheck.
9. After you are debt free, split your paycheck to have 40% automatically go into your "untouchable" savings/investing account.

What if you already earn less than your basic living expenses?

This is a very difficult situation and hard choices have to be made. Quite frankly, on some incomes and depending on what part of the country you live in, it's just not possible to save 40%. However, there is hope.

Increasing your income may be the only way. Here are some ways to do that and earn money fairly quickly.

- You can increase your income with a better job. Many of us qualify for scholarships and money for college to train for jobs that pay much more than we make right now.
- Start a side-job or business.
- Move to a home or to a city with substantially lower expenses. Many people are choosing a suburban or rural lifestyle over the hectic city life, and they are finding substantial financial savings in the process.

Budgeting To Pay Off Debt
By Gerri Detweiler

If you've set a goal to get out of debt then no doubt you're also trying to stick to a budget. The two go hand in hand. And though creating a budget that will allow you get out of debt sounds simple enough, getting there can feel like slogging through mud, on the side of a steep mountain no less. You probably feel like you're working as hard as you can and slowly making progress, then find yourself sliding right back down, perhaps where you started.

But getting out of debt is achievable. I've interviewed dozens of people from all walks of life who have collectively paid off hundreds of thousands of dollars in debt.

- Carrie Rocha and her husband paid off more than $50,000 in consumer debt.
- Julie Berry paid off more than $50,000 in credit card debt after her divorce, and went on to save an equal amount.
- MSgt Rachel Gause has paid off a similar amount as she works her way out of debt before she retires from the military.
- Beverly Harzog faced the embarrassment of having her maxed out credit cards rejected at the cash register before she decided to tackle her debt (especially mortifying since she was an accountant at the time),
- And Sandy Smith was faced with more than six figures in student loan and consumer debt after closing a business.

All of them are either debt-free or close to it. Their stories are both remarkable and mundane. None of them won the lottery or created and sold a high-tech start-up. Instead, they tackled their debt step by step, month by month. (You can read all their stories on the Credit.com blog).

One thing they all had in common was that they created a plan to get out of debt, and then stuck with it. But they didn't all take the same approach. And that's one reason they were successful.

Start At the Beginning

No matter which approach you decide to take, you can't begin to tackle your debt if you don't know how much you owe. You'll need a list of all your debts, the balances, and the interest rates along with the minimum payments required each month.

Your budget needs to accommodate your full car payment (if you have one) and your full mortgage or rent payment each month. But with credit cards, you have a little more leeway. You can pay the minimum payment, pay off the balance in full, or pay something in between. It's that last option that seems to trip us up most often. When money is tight, we may make the minimum payment. When we are feeling flush, we pay more. But often there's no rhyme or reason to our approach and as a result we become discouraged when we feel like we're making no progress. (Remember that muddy mountain path?) And then out come the credit cards.

Budgeting to pay back debt means committing to a payment plan. There's more than one way to accomplish this. Neither one is right or wrong; there are advantages and disadvantages to each approach. The best method is the method that works for you - and the one you will stick with.

Quick and Dirty

The simplest way to budget for debt payments is to look at your statements. Each of your credit card statements will list the amount you must pay each month in order to pay off your current balance in three years. Make a list of those three-year payment amounts. Can you pay that much each month for the next 36 months, without running up new debt? If not, that's a sign you should talk with a reputable credit counseling agency (more on that in the moment). But if those payment amounts seem realistic, then put them into your budget.

Put the cards away in a place where it's hard to get to them-- a safety deposit box, for example. Some people have frozen their credit cards in a block of ice instead. You can even put your payments on "auto pay," so they come directly out of your checking account. You won't have to think twice about it until they are paid off.

As far as your credit scores are concerned, it's best to leave accounts open. But if that's too much temptation, then close them. You can worry about your credit scores when you're out of debt.

You can stop right there if you want. Make those payments for three years, stop using your cards, and you'll celebrate your debt-free date in 36 months.

But if you're like most of us, life will throw up some obstacles in your path. You'll get laid off at work, or your child will get sick and your copays will be more than you bargained for. Your car will break down, or maybe it will be the fridge. And in those cases you'll need either need something to fall back on, or you'll fall back on the credit cards.

So try at all costs to squeeze at least a small amount of savings into your budget. Granted, most savings accounts pay nothing in terms of interest these days, and most credit cards charge pretty high rates. So logically, you're better off putting as much money toward your debt as possible and forgoing the savings. But when you have to charge a purchase on a credit card you are trying hard to pay off, you'll get discouraged and maybe decide you don't have the fortitude to climb that mountain after all. So even if it's $25 or $50 a month, try to out something each month into an emergency savings account that's not easy to get to.

Take It Up A Notch

If you manage to get through a few months of paying down your debt this way without running up new balances, then you can start considering ways to pay off your debt even faster. One way to do it is with what's known as the "snowball" method: you pay as much as possible toward the credit card with the highest interest rate while making minimum payments on the rest. Once the most expensive card is paid off, you take the amount you were paying toward that one and roll it down to the card with the next highest interest rate, and so on. Unless the interest rates on your credit card balances are pretty similar across the board, this method will usually save you money and help you get out of debt faster by eliminating the ones with the highest interest charges first.

However, this approach does require discipline because you're not paying the same amount each month. And that means you can easily fall into the temptation of paying less than you'd planned when your budget feels too restrictive. So think carefully about whether this approach is right for you. It may be helpful to "get in shape" first with three-year level payments first.

Another way to get out of debt faster is to lower the interest rates on your existing debts. Lower interest rates mean more of your payment goes toward paying off the amount you charged, rather than toward interest. One way to do this is to simply call your issuers and ask. Card issuers want to keep customers who pay interest, and so a simple phone call could land you a better deal. If it doesn't, another option may be to transfer a balance to a card with a lower interest rate.

Some card issuers are now offering balance transfers and 0% for as long as 18 months. But of course there is a trap: if you just make minimum payments for 18 months you'll be left with a balance at a much higher interest rate when the 0% offer ends. If you include this approach in your strategy, make sure you're paying enough to retire that balance when the introductory rate ends.

Finally, if you're having trouble making the numbers work, consider getting help from a credit counseling agency. In its Transparency Report (8th edition), Cambridge Credit Counseling noted that clients who enrolled in a debt management program reduced their average interest rate by almost 12% and their total average monthly payment by just over $172. In a DMP, the client makes a monthly payment to the counseling agency which then pays participating creditors.

Whatever plan you choose, you will likely experience setbacks and surprises. But that's not always a bad thing. Accepting them as a challenge and a learning experience can make you stronger. And the view from the top of that mountain will be worth it.

Budgeting Tools:
Prepaid Credit Cards
By Elaine Starling

Have you ever wished for a way to recoup some of the money you pay out for regular bills every month? Would you love to make money back whenever you pay the rent, make your car payment or cover your electric and gas bill? And why not include a simple process to help with budgeting too! Sound like a dream? It's not...it's a Prepaid Credit Card.

How do prepaid cards work?

Prepaid credit cards look just like debit or credit cards; they have the magnetic strip, chip, long number on the front and a familiar logo such as MasterCard or Visa.

Although looking the same as a credit or debit card (you even get your own PIN as you would for another card), a prepaid card does not let you spend from your current bank account, nor does it let you pay for goods by using a pre-agreed credit facility.
Instead it works on a simple premise: you load money on to the card (how much is up to you, although there's usually a minimum and maximum amount you can pre-load), and then you use the card to spend money in the same way you'd spend using a credit or debit card.

Once the money on the card runs out, you can't spend any more until you have loaded some more funds.
Because prepaid cards are associated with one of the major card networks -- Visa, MasterCard, Discover, American Express -- they can be used anywhere those cards can, whether it's to buy groceries at the supermarket, score merchandise on eBay or even pay bills online.

Prepaid debit cards can be used online or at brick-and-mortar locations to make purchases, pay bills or get cash at a point of sale or from an ATM.

Without linking to a bank account, a prepaid credit card allows you to do things that require a credit card, like rent a car or book a hotel room. Prepaid cards even come with account and routing numbers, so you can have your paycheck direct-deposited onto your card -- no more need to deal with the high fees from check-cashing businesses.

Prepaid cards are available to everyone, including those with poor or no credit. If your credit history is poor or nonexistent, or if your credit score is so low that a regular credit card issuer doesn't want to support you, a prepaid card may be the perfect solution since there's no credit check to qualify.

Since you can't spend beyond the loaded value, prepaid cards are a great budgeting tool for adults as well as teens, who can learn to use a card judiciously without the temptation of a spending spree.

Prepaid cards aren't a form of credit, so they have no effect, positive or negative, on an individual's credit scores, according to Anthony Sprauve, a spokesman for MyFICO.com, the credit score website. A prepaid credit card won't help you build credit, but it can keep you from making that big mistake with a credit card that can harm your credit for a long time.

Cards that are network-branded, which most are, get some consumer protections through the payment network whether it's Visa, MasterCard, American Express or Discover. Cards that are lost, stolen or fraudulently misused might be covered by deposit insurance or a zero-liability policy, as some companies extend this protection while others don't.

Besides the basic ability to make purchases with a card, prepaid cards offer a variety of other features. Most allow you to withdraw cash from an ATM; you receive a PIN number for that purpose. It's even possible to set up recurring payments for monthly bills and have them automatically be charged to your prepaid credit card.

Reloading is simple. Need to put more cash on your card? You have four options:
- transfer money from a bank account or financial institution
- have your employer direct-deposit your paycheck onto your card
- transfer money from a PayPal account or
- reload in a retail store like Wal-Mart or Walgreens.

Most credit card issuers make money on the interest you pay on your debt. With reloadable prepaid cards, the profit's in the fees. You can be hit with fees when you purchase the card (it's billed as a one-time "setup fee"), add more cash to your balance, withdraw money from an ATM or even check your balance online. Plus, many cards charge a monthly maintenance fee whether you're actively using the card or not.

Though fees are more the norm than the exception, every prepaid card has a different fee structure. A few offer fee-free transactions. Others waive fees when you carry a high-enough balance on your card, direct-deposit a paycheck, or cash checks at the retailer that sells the card.

Prepaid cards can help you manage your money.

With increased risk among consumers and conservatism among banks, the higher bar to qualify for a checking account is pushing a number of people toward prepaid cards. As a result, the use of prepaid cards rose by about 18 percent last year, according to a new study from Javelin Strategy and Research. "Because of the recession, people want better control of their money," says Beth Robertson, Javelin's director of payments research. "They want the ability to control their cash flow."

If you're an under-banked person and you have to pay your phone bill, you have to pay for a money order, then pay to send it out. For some people, the prepaid credit cards are truly a cost savings. Even for those with a regular bank account, a prepaid card can be a clever budgeting tool. Load your monthly grocery budget onto a prepaid card and use it strictly at the supermarket; when the money's gone, your spending stops automatically.

Prepaid cards offer some of the same theft and loss protections as a credit card. If you report the loss or theft of a registered card to the issuer, most will restore your original balance and issue a new card. Depending on the card, you also have some of the same protections offered by a bank, in that the amount on your card is FDIC-insured up to $250,000. That makes a debit card that acts like a credit card a fairly safe bet.

Who Uses Prepaid Credit Cards?

Prepaid debit cards began to take off in the 1990s as credit card companies realized that a significant portion of the U.S. population was not able to qualify for many of their credit cards. For the 80 million people in America who prefer not to deal with banks, a prepaid card can make life easier.

Uses of prepaid credit cards include general purposes, payroll, employee incentives, health care spending, government benefits, rebates and gifts. Government agencies use prepaid debit cards to disburse unemployment, welfare, workers' compensation and food stamps because making electronic deposits to plastic is cheaper than printing and mailing paper checks. It costs a couple of dollars to issue a check but only about 10 cents to deposit funds to a prepaid card.

Governments like prepaid credit cards because they save a lot of money. Beneficiaries like prepaid credit cards because they know the money is there at midnight on the day they're supposed to get it. They don't have to wait for the postman or take time away from their job to run over and cash a check.

Prepaid Cards, like any financial product, have their own unique advantages and disadvantages:

ADVANTAGES

- A prepaid card is given on the basis of your deposited money. So everyone is eligible - even those with bad credit. There are no credit checks, no employment verification and approval is guaranteed. However, you will still need to provide acceptable ID and be a US resident.
- Prepaid cards are as widely accepted as credit cards, and are even more accepted than credit cards in some cases. They can be used on the internet, on phone and all other vends.
- Prepaid cards are convenient and provide controllable spending power. You set your spending limit, not the card provider. All you need to do is top up your card when you need to via text, phone, a qualified retailer, the Post Office or via transfer from your bank account.

- Available to everyone, regardless of credit rating, income, or whether or not you hold a bank account.
- You can't get into debt. Your card stops working until you put more money on it. Since you can only spend what you have deposited, the chances of overspending are negligible. This can hugely increase financial discipline and help build good financial habits.
- Can function as a basic type of bank account. Prepaid accounts are an alternative to a traditional bank account and a new way to manage your money. With certain prepaid account cards for everyday use, there is no need for a bank account as they allow your wages to be paid onto your card and allow you to top up the amount whenever you wish.
- The activity and usage of your prepaid card can be tracked online or by using phone. This makes is super easy to control and monitor all your spending, generate reports and keep records.
- Prepaid cards can be used to pay utility and other bills online and by phone.
- Some prepaid cards provide cash back when you use - and refer a friend to use - the prepaid card as a credit card.

DISADVANTAGES

- There may be fees.
- Setting up a prepaid card.
- Loading money onto the card (try to only put money onto your card by bank transfer, as this method tends not to attract any fees).
- Monthly administration (although some providers offer a pay-as-you-go option).
- Making purchases on the card
- Taking cash out at a cash point.
- Inactivity. If you leave funds on your card, there is a possibility that they will be swiped off after a certain period of time. Other cards charge a fee if you don't use your card regularly.
- Redeeming funds fee. If you've got leftover cash on the card, and you want to extract it to avoid the inactivity fee, you may still get stung with a redemption fee.

- A prepaid card is not a credit card. Credit cards benefit from purchase protection by law, but prepaid cards don't have to offer this.
- Once your money is loaded onto a prepaid card, it isn't earning you interest as it would do in a bank account.
- There are certain transactions you can't use your Prepaid Card for; mainly transactions where your card would normally need to be pre-authorized before the full cost of your purchase is known.
- Also, if you have $99 on the card and you want to buy an item worth $100, you would need to load more money onto the card before you can buy, so it pays to plan ahead.

All in all, the advantages of prepaid debit cards usually outweigh the disadvantages -- especially for those individuals who don't have access to standard credit cards due to lack of credit history or because their credit rating is less than perfect.

The Prepaid Card that may revolutionize the field:

Women's Money® is always looking for innovative solutions to managing money easier. The Women's Money® Program is designed to help women have a place of support while they take action on their personal finances to create a strong foundation. Building a strong foundation is the first step to building a brighter future. That's why being resourceful in budgeting and spending habits is essential.

Changing the way women relate to finances requires a complete shift in women's attitudes and behaviors around financial health. Such a shift requires a holistic program that establishes lifelong habits for success. Women's Money continually researches the latest financial rules, tactics and tools that give you greater control over your money.

There is a new prepaid card which gives you cash back rewards while making it easy to manage your budget. Imagine - earning money every time you pay your bills, groceries, and fun!

It's simple to get a card since there is no credit check. There are no minimum balance requirements.

Your money is safe on the prepaid card because the funds loaded on the card are FDIC insured, so your money is always secure.

Paying cashback rewards isn't a secret formula; it's just math. When a business accepts your prepaid credit card as a credit card, the business pays a small fee called "interchange". This new upcoming card uses these fees to pay cashback rewards to cardholders who spread the word about the card.

How to Get the Money You Spend Back in Your Wallet:

To qualify for cash back rewards, you have to purchase $350 worth of goods and services per month using this prepaid card as a credit card and refer your friends who do the same. You probably already make this amount of purchases each month by purchasing groceries and gas on your existing debit, credit or prepaid card.

The key to getting most of all of that $350 you spend back into your bank account is the referral system.

Many of us are familiar with refer-a-friend rewards from companies like DirectTV, Chase, TMobile, Sprint, and many, many more. What's so cool about this prepaid cash back rewards is that they don't pay you back for referring a friend. They pay you a portion of what your friend spends on their card. It's not just a one-time referral fee. It's an on-going reward, and everyone involved wins.

The more friends you refer, the more you can earn in rewards (cold hard cash). Everyone you refer and everyone they refer (up to six levels beyond you) becomes your "Eligible Referral Group."

It's like a bull's eye where you are in the center and the people you refer are in the first ring.

The people in your first ring refer this prepaid card program to their friends who are put in your second ring; those in your second ring refer this prepaid card program to their friends who are put in your third ring, and so on for a total of six rings. You earn based on how many people in all six rings are using this prepaid card program so it's not dependent purely on your own spending.

For example, if you refer 3 people who each refer 3 people (then you have 9 people in your second ring of the bull's eye) who each refer 3 people (27 in your third ring) who each refer 3 people (81 in your fourth ring) who each refer 3 people (243 in your fifth ring) who each refer 3 people (729 in your sixth ring) which gives you a total of 1,092 people in your Eligible Referral Group.

For this example I used, your maximum cash back reward is $343.98 per month assuming that everyone in your Eligible Referral Group purchases $350/month using this prepaid card program as a credit card. In this example, you would earn almost 100% of your bill money back by participating in this prepaid card program. The cash back rewards can go higher. I just used the basic example here.

This prepaid card program offers a low fee structure too.

Features only this prepaid card program offers.

There are quite a few features that this prepaid card program offers that aren't offered with any other prepaid card or credit card:

Through their innovative cash back rewards system, you have the opportunity to earn some, all or more than what you purchase using the card. (Yes, I said more than what you spend).

While other pre-paid cards restrict your purchasing power by allowing you to load a maximum of only $500 per day and $5000 total on the card, This prepaid card program has a $5,000 per day loading limit and $10,000 total on the card.

If you have a bank account, you can link your card to your bank account.

You can get companion cards for your family.

Every time you use this prepaid card program, you are participating in a fundraiser that supports Women's Money programs.

Pre-Register for this card at
www.cascadecard.com/womensmoney.

This is not a product of Women's Money; however, Women's Money is using it and every time you purchase anything on this card, it raises money for the charity.

So here's how I see it:

Prepaid cards are a great budgeting tool and some are better than others. It depends on you, and the features that work for you and your family. The misconception is that all pre-paid credit cards are alike, and they clearly are not so shop around for the one that helps you most with your budgeting and spending needs.

Budgeting: Online Tools

- Monthly Spending Planner & Calculator via WomensMoney.org: If you are signed up for Program One Mentoring, We have several budgeting tools in the Education Center in Your Mentoring Portal
- MoneyMinderOnline.com
- Mint.com
- daveramsey.com/tools/budget-forms/
- kiplinger.com/tool/spending/T007-S001-budgeting-worksheet-a-household-budget-for-today-a/
- BudgetPulse
- BudgetTracker
- Buxfer
- Manilla.com
- PayDivvy.com
- BillMonk.com
- personalcapital.com
- gnucash.org
- moneytrackin.com
- youneedabudget.com
- savvymoney.com
- money.strands.com

Budgeting: Apps

- HomeBudget with Sync
- Spendbook
- YNAB
- Free Budgeting Apps
- Wally
- BillGuard
- Dollarbird
- Mint free
- Acorns free
- Robinhood free
- Ebates Coupons and Cash Back

Budgeting Tips:
44 Things to Consider
When Building a Budget

1. Be Realistic: Making your plan too strict doesn't help. You do still have to enjoy living, so be realistic about what makes you feel excited about life (shoes, movies, hiking, martinis, etc.). Cut the spending amount, but don't live without; otherwise, you'll end up on a spending spree that creates a depressive and regretful spending hangover.

2. Another Reality Check: Making a plan based on imaginary money you're going to make in the near future is a sure way to get into debt that you can't get out of. Get in the NOW. If you can't live on what you make now, you won't be able to manage when the raise or windfall comes in. Find Money Leaks: Are You Leaking? If you're budget is not adding up to match your budget, then there is a leak or two that you need to plug. Track your spending. Find it and adjust. For many people the main culprit is flexible spending like groceries and entertainment. The daily coffee habit is one thing, but to really get your budget in check, you need to figure out how much you're spending on the big things too. So get out some paper, and at the top, write down your total monthly income after taxes. Then write down what you spent on every bill this month including loans and credit cards. Divide each number into your income to determine the percentage you are spending for each expense (Example: You spend $725 on rent and make $2400 per month: 725/2400= 30%). Then compare those percentages to what experts recommend is the smartest way to divvy up your income:

3. Track Your Spending: It's always the inexpensive little daily purchases that really add up. Coffee, bagels, magazines, taxis. It's quite often an almost automatic, habitual, unconscious spending.

4.   Make Substitutions: You don't necessarily have to stop doing everything you love. Just find a better way to do it. If you love coffee, start making your own instead of dropping the money at a coffee shop.

5.   Go Old School: Sticking within a budget can be caused from too much automatic access to your money. The best way to stop the cash flowing from your bank account into someone else's is to pay yourself in cash and only use cash to pay for flexible expenses. The best way to not overspend is to carry cash whenever possible — out to dinner or to the grocery store, if you take out exactly what you have allotted for that outing you won't be splurging on anything else cause you won't have any more money to use

6.   Auto Save: If you are not great with transferring money into your savings account let the bank do it for you. Set up an amount you know you can save each month or paycheck and set up an auto transfer. You can always change it or cancel it for a period that you will need more money.

7.   Online or App Budgeting: Women's Money, Mint, MoneyStrands and You Need a Budget are all online and offer tips and classes to get you started.

8.   Use the 50/20/30 Guideline from Elizabeth Warren's book, "All Your Worth.": If you have more flexibility and discretionary income you may wonder where your money should be going. The answer is different for everyone. You may be in a hurry to pay off debt, so you're willing to spend less on eating out in the meantime. You might live in a city where rent is expensive, so you have to allocate more of your income to housing. Learnvest came up with a general benchmark to consider if you're just starting to set up a budget: the 50/20/30 guideline. Whether you're a parent with two kids or a recent college grad working your first job, this 50/20/30 guideline can help you not only figure out how much you may want to allocate to each area every month; it can also help you determine the order in which your money can be allocated. Budget a

maximum of 50% to fixed costs (rent, car payment, insurance, etc); a minimum of 20% to funding financial goals (savings, investing, etc); and a maximum of 20% to flexible spending (groceries, entertainment, etc). Budget your actual take home pay: If you can make pre-tax investments, savings, etc. this comes out of your paycheck before you apply your budget to your money. Same with taxes. Don't budget on your gross income. Budget on your net, take home pay.

9. Aim to spend no more than 90% of your income. That way, you'll have the other 10% left to save for your big-picture items. If you can figure out how to live on 80% or even 60% of your income, you will never be or feel poor.

10. Remember annual expenses: These are so easy to forget in your budget, and you find you have to steal from another budget item to pay for those annoying annual expenses, like licenses and car registrations. Calculate your full total of annual expenses. Pad it by 10% for fee increases. Then split that amount by 12 (months). Take that amount and put it automatically each month into a separate free checking or savings account that you pay annual bills out of.

11. Devise a plan that feels good, which only makes it easier to stick with.

12. Prepare the budget as a family with your spouse and children cooperating on the budget preparation. In this way, each would know where bulk of the expenses go and would try to make an effort to lessen those expenses considered as wants.

13. Add a "Murphy's Law" savings account for unexpected events that occur that aren't quite emergencies, but acts more like an "overdraft protection" account with no interest. The added bonus of budgeting is when you run out of money in a certain category (let's say gas for your car) you know you are not left in a lurch. Anything left in that account at the end of the month can go to your savings as a bonus payment.

14. Good old pencil and paper- sometimes if you have trouble budgeting it's just because your brain doesn't work well with online concepts. Maybe you are a person who needs to touch and feel the budget to make it real.

15. Free Excel workbook Within Your Means. Filling out the workbook is fairly easy, it's easy to update as you think of things omitted in the first pass, and you get a clear idea of the amount of money available to spend vs. the amount already committed. You can download it for free.

16. Set up set aside accounts (covered in the saving section of this book). It is a separate savings / checking account. You can have different categories such as dog, car insurance, car repair, life insurance, vacation, christmas, extra taxes (for self employment income), property taxes, home insurance, gifts and misc. Divide each bill by 12 and that amount is how much gets deposided each month. Some categories don't get a bill so guestimate the amount for the year. For instance Christmas, you can put $100 each month. Each month I put a designated amount in this account. Set up my set aside accounts at a different bank from the bank where your checking and regular savings accounts are so it is not easy to move money because in the beginning it's tempting to "borrow" from it.

17. Another thing to do and is most fundamental when it comes to doing **budget** is to reduce expenses to be able to set aside funds for savings and investments.

18. Track spending. Most people are spending significantly more than they budget.

19. Create a "fudge" factor into your **budget**. Set aside a smaller amount ($100 or so) each month for small emergencies, until you really got a grasp on our monthly expenses. Eventually, you won't need this $100 buffer any more, but it comes in handy. My favorite was the time that the windshield wipers flew off the car into a store parking lot.

20. Instead of budgeting based on my take-home pay, you may prefer to create a secondary budget that includes things that are deducted from your paycheck (like taxes, insurance premiums, and 401(k) contributions). It can give you a better picture of where all of your money is going.

21. Want more of a guideline of how to divide your expenses? There is no "right" way, but following this guideline could be helpful:

    1. Your base rent (not including utilities) should account for about 30% of your income.

    2. 10% should be spent on utilities and other necessary living staples, such as cleaning supplies and toilet paper.

    3. Student loans should account for 8% of your income.

    4. Credit cards, car payments and any other personal loans should come in between 10 and 20% of your income.

    5. Car insurance (or if you don't drive, your transportation costs) should account for 15%.

    6. 8% should go toward clothing and similar items.

    7. Food expenses (including eating out) should be no more than 18% of your income.

    8. You can spend up to 5% on recreation and entertainment.

    9. 10% goes into savings.

    10. If you add up all these percentages you'll get 114%, so clearly the experts are assuming you have most of these expenses but not all. So you'll have to juggle the numbers around to fit your needs. These percentages won't include all of your spending either, like the wedding present you had to buy for your cousin or the emergency new tire you needed when you got your flat. This means random expenses

will either have to come from your savings or you'll need to reduce

22. If you hate managing money and tracking it, partner, marry, or hire someone who loves it and whom you can easily communicate with...someone who will give you the overview without making you deal with the minutia.

23. Change your viewpoint. Make budget planning not only about how to save money but also about making plans on how to spend money.

24. It takes approximately 88 years to pay off $1000 by paying the minimum $10.00/month. That thousand dollars? In reality will turn into $10 560 at the end of those 88 years. It's not really a bargain at that point-- is it?

25. Spend on a credit card and pay it off every WEEK, in full. That way, if you're busy or miss a week, you can be sure it'll still get done and no fees will accrue. It also shows you VERY QUICKLY if you're heading toward over-budget. If I don't have enough on hand (i.e., in checking, not drawing from savings) to pay in full right then, it's time to tighten the belt for the coming week and get back on track.

26. Have a balance range [approx 2 months of bills] in your checking account. Any time the balance goes over the top end of the amount, put the money into savings.

27. Have an annual meeting to discuss your finances – everyone has their opinion and "buy in" with the budget methodology.

28. At that meeting, discuss your lives and your goals for those lives. Dream and discuss your priorities. It is good way to remind yourselves of your priorities and to adjust your spending to be sure it is in line with your priorities.

29. Tithe yourself. Aim to spend no more than 90% of your income. That way, you'll have the other 10% left to save for your big-picture items.

30. Don't count on windfalls. When projecting the amount of money you can live on, don't include dollars that you can't be sure you'll receive, such as year-end bonuses, tax refunds or investment gains.

31. Beware of spending creep. As your annual income climbs from raises, promotions and smart investing, don't start spending for luxuries until you're sure that you're staying ahead of inflation. It's better to use those income increases as an excuse to save more.

32. Once you have a budget, it's time to go through your spending and figure out where you need to cut back. This is especially urgent, but not uncommon, if you spend more than you make - a scary position. If your spending exceeds your income, then your top priority in constructing a budget should be to slash your spending, pronto.

33. The most common spending problems are caused by a house that's too large, a car that's too luxurious or a credit-card lifestyle that's too lavish for your income.

34. Over time, your income should rise as your career progresses and you manage to save money for investing. However, inflation will raise the cost of living. A mere 3% annual rise in prices will double the cost of everything within 24 years. So in 24 years, you'll need twice as much money as you do today to live your current lifestyle. Don't start spending your rising income on luxuries you've been denying yourself until you're sure that you're staying ahead of inflation.

Free Your Mind, Free Your Money
By Leisa Peterson, CFP®

We all feel out of sorts with money, from those of us struggling with debt to the successful business owners I work with on a weekly basis.

People are programmed to avoid things that cause them fear. Sure, we may pop into the movie theater to catch the latest horror flick, but when it comes to living our day-to-day lives, most of us go out of our way to avoid scary things.

Unfortunately for many, budgets are the things that go bump in the night.

Many of us have been taught to think of a budget as a weapon of mass destruction, a tool that sets us up for self-flagellation. The self-defeating thought process is often, "I'm going to set a budget and beat myself up if I can't keep to it, so I'm not going to do it at all." It is similar to a diet that you ignore and instead of altering your approach, you mentally destroy yourself as you reach for a doughnut or some candy.
That has to stop. We need to change our mental approach to finance.

I think of a budget as a diagnostic tool. It is no different from going to the doctor and having the nurse take your temperature and blood pressure. They are establishing a baseline for your health. A budget is a baseline for your financial wellness.

The doctor doesn't beat you up if you have high blood pressure. It is discovery. It gives the doctor the information needed to fix the problem. Look at a budget the same way -- it's diagnostic.

If a doctor told you to exercise regularly or reduce your sodium intake, you would listen. Well, I am not a doctor, and I don't play one on TV, but listen when I urge you to look at your soon-to-be-born budget a different way. It is not a setup for failure; it is a prescription for long-term success.

Creating a budget allows you to get an understanding of where your money is allocated and what changes will help you get what you most want out of life. That's right, creating a budget can cause happiness, not stress!

So how do you get started?

Before you get going on the nuts and bolts of creating a budget, I have found it very helpful to focus on shifting the mindset first. While changing your mind is not always easy, it is possible, and you can start by following these four steps:

#1 Be Aware. Before we can make any significant changes in our lives, we need to become aware of our money challenges. We need to look at them for what they really are, even if they are not pretty (and they often aren't!). When we really allow ourselves to feel a bad feeling for what it is, we usually want to get rid of it more than we want to keep holding onto it. That is when we'll know were ready to start making some changes.

One example is the realization of the discomfort experienced when avoiding things like filing taxes by April 15th. Instead of taking care of the issue in a timely way, prolonging the problem causes greater stress later on, not to mention financial penalties. Becoming aware of the habitual approach taken when it comes to money responsibilities allows us to feel whatever we are resisting and see that it isn't as bad as we thought.

#2 Accept What Is. Acceptance has to come from deep inside even if that means feeling uncomfortable. By allowing our feelings to exist and giving ourselves permission to experience pain, we open the door to acceptance.

Money often brings up feelings of guilt, shame, greed, anger and frustration, which are all emotions we work very hard to avoid feeling. Understanding our natural resistance to these feelings is useful, as it takes the emotional charge out of the resistance and allows us to think more objectively. Seeing how whatever we resist has a funny way of persisting helps us to step back and accept what is. It may have felt like avoidance was the safest option in the past when it came to money, however as we shift into acceptance, we see how important it is to have a way to diagnostically understand our money and our feelings about it.

#3 Allow Change to Occur. When we diffuse our emotions, we are able to step back and shift our attention towards discovering the deeper cause of our feelings. This allows us to recognize our money patterns, as well as the root cause of our avoidance. I have used this process for years, as it helps get to the bottom of why we do the things we do. Avoiding money-planning tools often connects into fears of not having enough. Once we discover our secret feelings, we can recognize that while this may have been a past tendency, it doesn't have to be our long-term reality. Seeing that change is not only a possible but necessary step for taking responsibility for our own happiness allows us to realize how budgeting can be a great way to learn about the numbers and our personal tendencies at the same time.

#4 Taking Action. By the time you arrive at this step, there will be much less resistance to creating and maintaining a livable budget (or whatever you wish to call it). In fact, you may feel a sense of excitement because you see that your old way of thinking has shifted into wanting to create your own path to success by harnessing greater control of your money. Using the budget as a diagnostic tool makes a lot of sense and is clearly the best way to move forward.

Knowing where you are with your money helps you take action if and when change is necessary, so you can live proactively versus reactively.   Too little money coming in represents an opportunity to either cut expenses or to earn more money. In fact, I have met several people who had so much fun being creatively frugal that they actually made businesses out of their hobby, proving that you never know what may come from changing your mindset.

One client I worked with to create a budget realized she was running a deficit every month of several hundred dollars which was causing her to increase her debt load substantially. By proactively controlling some of her expenses, she was able to not only stop adding to her credit card debt, she found ways to begin paying it down which led to less stress and less impulse spending. She also decided to start a side business selling jewelry which gave her the opportunity to splurge from time to time. In the end, she found that having a budget made life a lot easier and more enjoyable because when you know the facts about your money, anything is possible.

So now you have some ideas for shifting your mindset so that budgeting becomes easier and more enjoyable. Seeing it as a diagnostic tool, rather than a painful weapon, places you in control of your money rather than it being in control of you. By following these tips, you can easily create a livable budget, one that will help you achieve peace of mind and get rid of many financial worries.

Spending Your Money

Spending: Strategies & Concepts

Spending beyond your limits is dangerous. But if you do, you've got plenty of company. Government figures show that many households with total income of $50,000 or less are spending more than they bring in. This doesn't make you an automatic candidate for bankruptcy - but it's definitely a sign you need to make some serious spending cuts.

Where Does All My Money Go?

Excerpt from the Women's Money® Guidebook -
for the full chapter, join the Women's Money Mentoring program.

Follow the Money

The old saying of "follow the money" is usually something you'd hear in spy mystery movie, but the same advice holds true for your own personal finance "mystery". **Knowing your net worth and your budgeting numbers are important, but knowing this alone is not enough.** You need to also know where your money goes on a weekly, monthly and annual, basis. Some people keep very close records and know where every penny goes. Other people rely on their monthly bank statements to give them an idea of where their money has gone. There are several methods to track spending. Over time, you will develop methods that suit your style comfortably without feeling overburdened by the task.

Before you can engage in good financial planning for the future, you have to assess where your money is going today and every day. Keep in mind that how you spend money can vary each day. The ways you spend your money include cash or debit card, check, and credit card. Some people also have electronic accounts, such as Pay Pal, but such accounts are normally associated with a primary checking account.

Why is it important to write down every amount that is spent, even the smallest cash sums? Because it is the only sure-fire way of knowing what you have done with your money. You cannot make successful financial plans for the future without knowing your spending history.

There's an App for That

There are also several free apps to track your spending such as Budget Buddy, My Budget Free, Lumen Trails (free version), and many other money tracking apps are available. Find one that works for you.

More Cool Tools

On the next page you'll find the "Money Finder". You can make copies this page or download and print copies from your computer by getting the document from your Program One Mentee Education Center (accessible through your Online Mentoring Portal).

Also available for free download in your Mentoring Portal's Education Center:

- Money Finder System Calculator – it automatically calculates your weekly and monthly spending totals for you.
- Money Spending and Planning Calculator – this combines the Money Finder System with your Monthly Spending Plan (budget). With this tool you can put in your budget and enter your actual spending to see how they compare. It automatically calculates your weekly and monthly spending totals for you.

Getting a handle on post break up spending...
By Mikelann Valterra

You just broke up. Perhaps your marriage ended or your boyfriend moved out. And you find yourself suddenly having to spend less....

Thinking about your new life when you are hurting from relationship loss can be overwhelming. When you factor in the financial stress that intrudes on top of the grief and general chaos, it may feel like too much to bear. As a money coach, I've sat with many women in this situation. Often, both income and expenses have changed. Perhaps you've suddenly become a one income household. Or, you are the one moving out and your expenses are completely different.

It can feel like a cruel aftershock to find you can't spend in the way you've become accustomed. It feels unfair – adding insult to injury. No wonder many women feel like a deer caught in the financial headlights once a relationship ends.

You may know you need to spend less at a transition period like this – at least temporarily while regaining a sense of balance. But your mind seems determined to encourage you to spend, spend, spend!

What the heck is that about?

We are emotional beings, and this comes out in our spending. To pretend that we should "suck it up" and "just get a handle on things" is to deny that we are human. Money is emotional. And nowhere does it get more emotional than right after a break up.

So how do you get a handle on your spending?

Emotional spending post-break up

The reality is that we all spend emotionally from time to time. We spend when we are happy and also to make us feel better. "Retail therapy" both entertains us and lifts our spirits – at least in the moment. We all know that feeling of regret when the credit card bill comes in or when we don't have enough in our account to pay our other bills. Then we rush to beat ourselves up. Many even leave the mall already feeling stressed, anxious and regretful about their recent purchase.

But in the moment, spending distracts us and soothes us so we keep doing it.

And this is never truer, or more detrimental, than right after a big break up.

For some of us, it's quite possible that we already knew we had a tendency to overspend. Possibly, spending too much when we were depressed, anxious or bored. Or perhaps we knew we overspent and it caused issues in our lives, like debt and relationships stress, but we were never sure what to do about it.

And now this overspending tendency may be on overdrive, right at a point when you desperately need to get a handle on it.

Even if you've never identified with being an overspender, it's quite possible that you are feeling very raw and emotional about money currently, and spending money is "feeling" scary right now. So how do we look squarely at this and take care of ourselves, emotionally AND financially? Understanding the root of the problem is a good start.

Break ups suck – give me more of that feel-good chemical
There is a lot that goes on in the moment of spending money on something we enjoy, such as clothes. An actual "feel-good" chemical (dopamine) gets released in our brain when we spend money on something fun and new for us. Feeling really good as we anticipate buying something, or feeling fabulous in the moment of purchase, literally releases this chemical in our brains. This is part of having a normal, healthy brain.

So feeling good (or almost "high") as you spend money on things you enjoy is not your imagination. And when we are suffering from a recent break up, it's natural that we would seek even more of this feel-good chemical to combat the blues of a break up.

If this sounds like you, know that you are normal! Most of us do spend emotionally from time to time, and if you've just gone through a break up, your brain and soul are literally aching to feel better.

And, it may be time to think about other ways to combat the blues.

Are you in therapy to support you in this post break up time? Do you want to talk to your therapist or your doctor about benefiting from an anti-depressant for the time being? Are you walking and exercising? Are you seeing your women friends enough? How can you get those feel-good chemicals to course through your brain?

One thing that lifts our spirits is having something to look forward to. We relish having something to think about and plan, almost as much as the actual event. So saving money for a weekend trip with a fun friend may ultimately be cheaper than multiple trips to the mall. (This assumes you don't hit the mall on your trip...)

The point is to realize that you are likely down. And using shopping as the antidote to the blues, while temporarily effective, can be particularly harmful in a post-break up situation. So acknowledge that you are down and think about other ways to combat it. You deserve support during this time. When I divorced, I spent countless hours in the bathtub, soaking and reading. I watched 20 episodes of some TV shows I missed....you know...all in one weekend. I spent a lot of time with my women friends. And therapy? Oh yes.

Connecting more with women friends: the conundrum

We all love our friends, but let's be real here, they can be pricey sometimes. Women spend more when they are with friends, and they also spend money ON their friends buying gifts and thoughtful items. This is the joy of being a woman! And during a break up, we need our women friends more than ever....can you see the conundrum coming?

You need your friends, but it can be financially disastrous if all of your connection time with friends is spent shopping. We are already prone to overspend as we fight the blues, and shopping with other people exacerbates our urge to spend.

So, as you are healing, you need to find ways to connect with your friends that don't involve spending money. Can you invite them to dinner? If you don't cook, even going out to dinner can cause less financial damage then wandering the mall with them. Can you meet for a walk, or a monthly manicure?

Note: the goal is not to spend zero money. That is impractical and just not realistic. Rather, the goal is to feel in control of your spending as you assess your new reality and think through the new lifestyle you are creating as a happy single woman.

And part of healing, as women, is to spend serious time with our friends (not always being serious, of course). So think carefully about what you are doing when you are with your friends.

Reality check: Are you asking yourself right now, "We have always gotten together to go shopping, what if my friends don't want to hang out with me now? I can't lose them too!" Just know a true friend will understand your need to spend less money for a while, while you figure out what works in your new life. Simply saying, "I need to spend less for a while, so can we find less expensive restaurants, or skip the mall?" will be more than enough explanation for most people. Don't believe me? Think of this in reverse. If you had a friend come to you and say, "I need you! Can I come over??" you would rush to open your arms. And if she said she also needed to spend less while she figured things out, you would totally understand. Of course you would. And so will they.

Reconsidering your shopping entertainment habit

Many of us have formed a habit of shopping as entertainment. This is related to both how good it can feel (hello dopamine!) and also how enjoyable it is to be with friends. But there is also a simple entertainment component to shopping.

You may shop alone. In fact, it can be about needing to be alone (take a break from your kids, your house, and your work). It can be about the thrill of hunting for a good deal. It can be around shopping for a particular hobby. Or to shore up self-esteem and buy the clothes that will make you feel more beautiful.

No wonder so many of us enjoy shopping.

But why do we really shop? What is the underlying need we are trying to meet? Until you identify these needs you will have a hard time healing and moving on, so thinking through these real needs is key.

If you are striving to be alone, how can you meet this need? What else can you do that gets you out of the house? Can you take yourself to a movie? If you love the thrill of the hunt, can you satisfy this need at the thrift store? If your self-esteem needs some fluffing, can you invite a girlfriend over to help you put together three outfits that she thinks would look fabulous on you? Shopping does fulfill different needs we have, it's true. And it's why sometimes it turns into a habit. If shopping is just "what you do" when you've got some time and you want to go enjoy yourself, it is possible that it has become a habit.

If this is true, it's time to find some alternate entertainment. And this has to be a conscious decision. It won't just happen by itself (I know, it's a bummer). Because let's face it, heading to the mall out of habit and then trying to not spend money, while you are feeling sad, is like that science experiment you did in 5th grade with the baking soda in the volcano – a disaster waiting to happen. Don't do this to yourself. There is willpower and then there is putting yourself in a situation that simply isn't smart. Be nice to yourself. Find different entertainment.

The good news is that making a conscious decision doesn't have to be hard. What else can you do that is FUN?

Personal story time

When I divorced, I found myself spending a lot of money on the nights I did not have my son. I was adjusting to having a parenting plan and it was very strange, so I filled this new time...I was lonely and at loose ends. I found I could easily "entertain" myself at the mall and that is what I did. For a time I wandered the mall on my "kid-free" nights, looking to make myself feel better with a random purchase. I walked around and aimlessly spent money. I bought clothes to make me feel better, new bedroom linens, a little jewelry…

Eventually, my wallet started to cry. I knew I needed to feel better, and this shopping entertainment was starting to have some repercussions. And I was getting bored spending all that time by myself! So I called my women friends and finally convinced one to take a pottery class with me. I had spied one in the catalog of "no-credit" classes at the local community college down the street from my place.

For two months we laughed and made a lot of oddly shaped bowls and pots. By the end of that time, I felt calmer.

If you need a mood-lifter, can you throw a game party in your living room? If you need to be alone, go get a manicure? That will likely be less expensive than the mall. And it may make you feel more attractive too (yes!). Host an evening in with your friends and watch your favorite program (Downton Abbey, anyone?).

What about you? What ideas do you have to make yourself feel better, see your friends more and not spend a lot of money?

Now is the time to assess how you entertain yourself. And if you had a shopping habit in your old life, it's the perfect time to find new forms of entertainment that suit your new life.

Living consciously

What is the first step to living consciously? Don't panic. You will get through this, and it's quite possible that you will be even happier on the other side once the dust settles. For now, you need to reduce your stress and possibly your spending. And, you need to take care of yourself at a deep level. This reduction in spending may only be temporary, but it may give you some financial breathing room while you assess what is next.

Simply saying, "I have to spend less so I'm going to stop spending" is likely not going to work without a thoughtful look at how and why you shop. You are in a vulnerable place. You are likely hurting and need to feel better. You really need your friends. You probably need some distraction or time away from your children. Heck, you want and need to go out and entertain yourself! So don't pretend this is not true. It just won't work. Trust me.

Breaking up is hard and painful. This is the time to increase your self-care. But shopping, while it may be soothing in the moment, is usually not the answer.

Once you put a name to your triggers and think about how to really, truly take care of yourself, you can begin to find other ways to care for yourself that are both fun and nurturing.

Your new, conscious, life awaits.

Good Deals, Like Good Relationships, Take Time to Develop
By Kathleen Bellucci

If you use the tools that are available to you, there are no more excuses for you to allow any decisions to be made without completely understanding them.

Check before you write a check.

DON'T RUSH THIS PROCESS!

If you do your homework then when you sit down to discuss your options, you already have an arsenal of questions. If that advisor doesn't have the answers you seek, move onto another. NEVER be afraid to end an appointment that isn't providing what you came for. You time is just as valuable. Once you feel that you are being pressured to make decisions, you still don't understand your options after requesting information or just being "TALKED AT". Simply stand up, and let them know that you don't feel this relationship is what you are looking for. This may sound rude to you because of the way you were raised, but my philosophy on this topic has drastically changed as I learned to value my time as much as I value someone else's. Also, I now demand a professional to provide the information I seek and if they don't or can't, then my time with them is over. It will get easier to act this way because working with advisors who can positively impact your life is what you deserve. There is many advisors who can positively impact your financial future. Take the time to find the right one for you.

The beautiful thing about the world we live in is competition. There will always be someone else competing for your business. Don't give it away so easy, make them earn it. My father always told me that loyalty and trust is earned not given! You shouldn't trust without asking a lot of questions. You should interview an advisor just like you would a babysitter or house sitter or anyone you would trust your most prized possessions with. You need to start thinking of your money as a prized possession. Without it you are at a loss. Learn how to protect it better by requiring those that impact its success to provide the information that you need to protect it the best way you know how. You shouldn't be pressured to sign anything at your first visit with anyone. Sometimes we allow the time constraints of our life to do things we wouldn't normally do if we had more time. When it comes to your money, don't sign contracts, instructions or commitments of any kind in order to "save time" and get it over with. Take the information you are provided, research it some more and think about it before making any decisions. This should be a long term relationship and considered carefully. When I say anything, I mean anything that you spend your money on. I used this tactic after one of my cars literally blew up. I had two young kids and desperate for another car, but this was a 5 year commitment and I wasn't going to play the car dealership game until I was sure I could win. So I borrowed someone else's car during the "research" period and it worked out. I researched every website I could find and I went into 3 different dealerships. I had pulled my own credit report, I pulled the blue book price for both retail and wholesale and I learned what type of loan I could qualify for, what interest rate I should pay and what ultimate price I would accept walking out of the door. I met the salesman, put my watch on the table along with my folder of information and told him he had 15 minutes to negotiate this car with me or I was moving onto the next dealership. I left the dealerships empty handed but one of them called me back and I bought a car for what I believed was the best deal.

If you are willing to walk away from anything, you are more than likely to wind up with the best deal.

Think about it, would you have just married the first guy who came around because they were referred to you?
Good relationships take time to develop.

Decisions regarding financial relationships should be treated in the same manner.

Don't settle!

Organize Your "Other" Money!

By Brenda Prinzavalli, excerpt from 31 Days to an Organized Life!

Gift Certificates, Gift Cards, Credit Receipts, Coupons

You likely received at least one Gift Card for a gift, thank you or from returning a gift and receiving store credit. This is a good time to make sure you have an organized way to keep track of them.

This is your MONEY! Coupons or Discount Certificates can also fall into this category as they are money in your pocket if you shop or dine with a retailer offering a coupon! Find one safe and easy-to-remember location for these items.

The three main categories with this type of gift or money is to remember:

- that you have them,
- when they expire and
- where you have stashed them.

One idea is to simply put them in an envelope or a file folder labeled Gift Certificates, Gift Cards, Credit Receipts. If you have too many to look through on a regular basis, here are some possible ways to divide them.

- By the category; Food, Clothing, Personal Services, Office Stores, Misc
- By the type; Gift Cert, Gift Card, etc
- Alphabetical by store
- By expiration date. Not the top choice, but it might be the one that works for you.

Spending: Tools

- Walmart Savings Catcher: Enter or scan your receipt. Enter your receipt number or scan the barcode by downloading the Walmart App. App compare prices. Walmart will match the price of any local competitor's printed ad for an identical product. You get the difference. If Savings Catcher finds a lower advertised price, you get the difference. FREE.
- Ibotta: Ibotta allows shoppers to earn real money for shopping. Start by perusing the different offers in the product gallery and choose the ones you're interested in. Every time you compete a "task" (like sharing on Facebook, taking a poll, or watching a video), pending cash is added to your account that can be accessed once you actually purchase the product from one of the 50 retailers partnered with Ibotta. Once the purchase is verified, cash is put into your PayPal account or turned into gift cards. Available for: iOS and Android
- RetailMeNot: "Thousands of coupons in your pocket." Browse coupons and deals from hundreds of retailers. Save the coupons you want to use for easy access and get notifications for coupon expiration dates. You can also search for deals at the nearest stores. Don't worry about printing the coupons; all you have to do is show your phone at the register. Available for: iOS and Android
- SnipSnap: Like RetailMeNot, however, this one also lets you take pictures of printed coupons from many retailers and turns them into digital, mobile-ready ones. You can also browse the online directory and see the coupons that friends have "snipped." Available for: iOS
- Grocery iQ: Stay on task and avoid impulse purchases with this incredibly detailed grocery shopping list platform. Not only can you build grocery lists by searching through the millions of products in the app's database, but you can use voice recognition or barcode scanning. Grocery iQ also has a store locator feature and offers coupons. This app is a must-have for busy families or for anyone trying to keep their grocery budget under control. Available for: iOS and Android

- SavingStar: SavingStar is a digital coupon app for thousands of grocery stores and drugstores that is linked to your individual store loyalty cards. (you have to have loyalty cards to get rewards.) You choose the digital coupons you want to use and the reward is applied to your loyalty card and when you reach $5 in savings, you earn cash! You can even opt for your cash savings to go towards donations for the charity American Forests.Available for: iOS and Android
- Groupon: Redeem Groupon deals (as much as 50-90% off!) on everything from restaurants to retailers to hotels. You can search by location to find deals closest to you. Available for: iOS, Android, and Windows
- LivingSocial: Similar to Groupon, you can use this app to gain hand-held access to all of LivingSocial's deals.. An added bonus: if you share a discount you received on your social media accounts and three of your friends purchase the same deal, you'll get yours free of charge! Available for: iOS, Android, and Windows
- GasBuddy: Gas prices can be a major headache, but with GasBuddy, you can find the cheapest gas prices closest to you! Additionally, for every gas price you report, you earn points towards winning the weekly $250 prize for gas. With over 32 million visitors, the app remains extraordinarily up-to-date on your best gas deals. Available for: iOS, Android, Blackberry and Windows
- mySuperList: This app is incredible. Whether you do you food shopping online or in store it allows you to make a saving. You can create your shopping list while out and about and then check which supermarket is selling all of those items for the cheapest price. You can also get cashback on certain items with the app meaning even bigger savings. It's a no brainer really. Available for: iPhone Price: Free.
- Idealo: Do you hate buying something on a shopping trip only to find you could have bought it cheaper elsewhere? Idealo is a life saver for anyone who is caught out by making impulse purchases. Just scan the products barcode or enter the keywords to find how much you could get it for from retailers. You can download it here. Great bargaining tool! Available for: iPhone Price: Free.

- Expensify: This app offers both smartphone and web interfaces. The clean, easy-to-navigate interface features four big buttons: SmartScan, Add Expense, Track Time and Track Distance. Available for: iOS, Android & Windows Price: Free.
- Dailybudgt: DailyBudgt (yes, there's no 'e') is designed to help you keep track of your daily expenses. First, go into the app and set your budget for the week, then set your budget just for today. This can be especially useful if you're taking out an amount of cash as a method of slowing down your spending. You can also turn on a reminder for extra notifications about what you've spent from your daily and weekly budget. If you look at spending by week, you'll see the icons associated with each type of spending in addition to a smaller pie chart. Available for: iPhone Price: $1.99.
- Dailycost: DailyCost is an easy-to-use and rather basic app for tracking monthly spending. Enter your daily expenses, filing them under a variety of categories including movies, travel, books and groceries. DailyCost keeps track of everything through a counter at the top of the screen, organizing by number of days, number of entries and total cost. Available for: iPhone Price: $1.99.
- Hbl Moneywise: MoneyWise is designed to help you balance your budget, track expenses, generate reports and bank on the go through a "find ATM" option and mobile banking. Available for: iOS, Android Price: Free.
- Dollarbird: Dollarbird is a useful and intuitive money-tracking app that doesn't offer a lot of bells and whistles. This app uses a monthly calendar format, which allows you to look at how much you've spent every day of the month. Dollarbird also offers optional PIN code protection. Available for: iOS, Android Price: Free.

Spending:

100 Ways to Spend Less

1. Turn off the television: One big way to save money is to watch less television. Less temptation from ads to purchase things you think you need, less electrical use, and so on. Seek another hobby to unwind in the evening.

2. Turn a critical eye to your collections and hobbies. Most people collect something, but is it something that consistently brings you joy? Or is it something that you just do out of habit? Could you perhaps cut down on your spending on that hobby? Focus on trimming the things you don't feel strongly about, and find additional hobbies that are free.

3. Follow the thirty day rule. Whenever you're considering making an unnecessary purchase, wait thirty days and then ask yourself if you still want that item. Quite often, you'll find that the urge to buy has passed and you'll have saved yourself some money simpley by waiting.

4. Make your own gifts instead of buying stuff from the store. You can make food mixes, candles, bread, cookies, soap, and all kinds of other things at home quite easily and inexpensively. These make spectacular gifts for others because they involve your homemade touch.

5. Write a list before you go shopping – and stick to it. Never go into a store without a strong idea of what one will be buying while in there. Make a careful plan of what you'll buy before you go, then stick strictly to that list when you go to the store. Practice not putting anything in the cart that's not on the list, no matter how tempting.

6. Invite friends over instead of going out. Almost every activity at home is less expensive than going out. Invite some friends over and have a cookout or a potluck meal, then play some cards and have a

few drinks. Everyone will have fun, the cost will be low, and the others will likely reciprocate not long afterwards.

7. Don't spend big money entertaining your children. Most children, especially young ones, can be entertained very cheaply. Buy them a box for 76 cents and let their creativity run wild. Make a game out of ordinary stuff around the house, like vacuuming or tossing laundry into the washer. Realize that what your children want most of all is your time, not your stuff.

8. Buy video games that have a lot of replay value – and don't acquire new ones until you've mastered what you have. Focus on games that can be played over and over and over again, and focus on mastering the games that you buy. Good targets include puzzle games and long, involved quest games – they maximize the value of your gaming dollar.

9. Drink more water. Not only does drinking plenty of water have great health benefits, water drinking has financial benefits, too. Drink a big glass of water before each meal, you won't eat as much, saving on the grocery and entertainment bill. You'll also find yourself feeling a bit better as you begin to get adequately hydrated (most Americans are perpetually somewhat dehydrated).

10. Cut back on the convenience foods – fast foods, microwave meals, and so on. Instead of eating fast food or just nuking some prepackaged food when you get home, try making some simple and healthy replacements that you can take with you. If you don't know or like to cook, try making "raw" food snacks. They are the healthiest you can make and they charge a bundle at the health food store for items you can make in five minutes with a food processor.

11. Give up expensive habits, like cigarettes, alcohol, vaping, and drugs. Those habits cause money to flow away from you with nothing in return.

12. Free books and DVDs: Swap books, music, and DVDs cheaply on the internet via services like

PaperBackSwap or go to the Library or even try Craigslist for free stuff.

13. Buy appliances based on reliability, not what's cheapest at the store. It's worth the time to do a bit of research when you buy a new appliance. A reliable, energy efficient washer and dryer might cost you quite a bit now, but if it continually saves you energy and lasts for fifteen years, you'll save significant money in the long run. When you need to buy an appliance, research it. An hour's worth of research can easily save you hundreds of dollars.

14. Hide your credit cards. Take your credit cards and put them in a safe place in your home, not in your wallet where it's easy to spend them. Don't keep plastic on you until you have the willpower to not use it even when you're sorely tempted.

15. Plan your meals around what's on sale. Instead of just planning your meals based on a cookbook or whatever you can dream up, plan all your meals around what's on sale in your grocery store's flyer.

16. Don't claim allegiance to one store. Do a price comparison – and find a cheaper grocery store. Most of us get in a routine of shopping at the same grocery store, even though quite often it's not the one that offers the best deals on our most common purchases. Fortunately, there's a simple way to find the cheapest store around.

17. Challenge yourself to try making your own things. Making bread is easy now with breadmakers. Making pasta is actually relaxing. Making your own peanut butter takes only five minutes.

18. Create a refrigerator salad bar. If you are a victim of overspending on eating out, the easiest way to solve this is to take 10 minutes every week or few days to create a salad bar in your fridge. Purchase all your favorite salad makings and dressings. Chop and put each ingredient into a separate bowl. Estimate what you might need for the week. Next time you look in the fridge for something fast to eat, dole yourself up a big salad with a hand full of lettuce and then choose your toppings, premade. It literally takes less than five minutes to make a cobb

salad this way or whatever your favorites are. Using a cobb salad as an example though: Restaurant or fast food salad of this type will cost you $6-$15. Cobb salad in five minutes from your homemade salad bar will cost you about $2.

19. Don't spend money just to de-stress. Instead of spending to de-stress, try some basic meditation techniques, stretching, or yoga, walking, or going to the gym.

20. When shopping for standard items (clothes, sports equipment, older games, etc.), start by shopping used. Quite often, you can find the exact item you want with a bit of clever shopping at used equipment stores, used game stores, consignment shops, and craigslist and freecycle.org.

21. Remove your credit card numbers from your online accounts. It's easy to spend online when you have your card information stored in an account – just click and buy. The best way to break this habit is to simply delete your card from the account. When you're tempted to spend, you'll be forced to spend the time to dig out your card, and think about why you're spending this money.

22. Do holiday shopping right after the holidays.. Wait until about two days after a holiday when holiday items are 75% off, then go out shopping for items you need that are themed for that day. It works the same for other holidays too. Get a Mother's Day card for next year the day after Mother's Day. Get Easter egg decorating kits the day after Easter.

23. Join up with a volunteer program. It's a great way to meet new people, get some exercise, and involve yourself in a positive project that can lift your spirit. Most people spend out of boredom, so get up off your couch and do something good for the world. You'll feel better and more fulfilled than shopping can ever provide.

24. Try generic brands of items you buy regularly. Instead of just picking up the ordinary brand of an item you buy, try out the store brand or generic version of the item. Likely, you'll save a few cents now, but you'll also likely discover that the store

brand is just as good as the name brand – the only difference between the two, often, is the marketing.

25. Make the rounds first. If you like to go, or are in the habit of going, to the shopping center for entertainment, the n walk the mall first. Stop at every store. Really look at the window. Does anything really appeal to you? If something does, make note to come back to that store after you've done your "rounds". Do not go into any store until you've walked the ENTIRE MALL at least once. Two to three rounds are even better. The appeal of purchasing gets less with each round, you've mentally entertained yourself just as much as shopping, and you've gotten some exercise. You'll find that unless you really love something or need something, you lose the motivation to go into the stores that really don't meet your needs.

26. Before you buy, review your cart. Go into an aisle of the store where you can take a minute to think and review. Look at every item you are purchasing. Pick it up. Hold it. Ask yourself, why you want to purchase this. If the answer is "because it's cute", you probably better put it back because you probably have a lot of cute things. Determine if it's a need or want, and put the wants back.

27. Create a visual reminder of your debt. Make a giant progress bar that starts with the amount of debt you have and ends with zero. Each time you pay down a little bit, fill in a little more of that progress bar. Keep this reminder in a place where you'll see it often, and keep filling it in regularly. It keeps your eyes on the prize and leads you straight to debt freedom.

28. Eat breakfast. Eating a healthy breakfast fills you up with energy for the day and also decreases your desire to eat a big lunch in the middle of the day. Not only that, breakfast can be very healthy, quick, and inexpensive.

29. Don't fear leftovers. Have you ever seen the show "Chopped"? Play your own dinner game of taking leftovers and creating a whole new dish.

30.   Shop your closet. Go through your clothes – all of them. If you have a regular urge to buy clothes, go through everything that you have and see what you might find. Take the clothes at the back of the closet and bring them to the front and suddenly your wardrobe will feel completely different. Take the clothes buried in your dresser and pull them to the top. You'll feel like a brand new person who doesn't need to spend money on clothes right now.

31.   Brown bag your lunch. Instead of going out to eat at work, take your own lunch. Remember that salad bar idea? Pack a salad for work. Many people report saving $200 a month by deciding to bring a peanut butter and jelly sandwich for lunch to work. That's $2400 a year saved by the American classic.

32.   Learn how to dress minimally. Buy clothes that mix and match well and you'll not need nearly as many clothes. If you have five pants, seven shirts, and seven ties that all go together, you have almost an endless wardrobe right there just by mixing and matching. Accessorize with jackets and scarves to make it look like a different outfit.

33.   Get a mentor or support system. Ask for help and encouragement from your inner circle. Sit down and talk to the people who care and ask them for help. Tell them that you're trying to trim your spending and you'd love it if they offered any suggestions and support they might have, and try their advice before discounting their advice.

34.   If something's broken, see if repairing it is cheaper than replacing it. Sometimes buying new is the same or less than a repair, and other times repairs are cheaper. If you have a home warranty, it is quite often cheaper to repair home appliances, and with a good policy they may replace it at no extra charge if it unfixable.

35.   60. Check out what your town's parks and recreation board has to offer. My town has several wonderful parks, free basketball and tennis courts, free disc golf, trails, and lots of other stuff just there waiting to be used. You can go have fun for hours out in the wonderful outdoors, playing sports, hiking on

trails, or trying other activities – and it's all there for free. All you have to do is discover it.

36. Air up your tires. For every two PSI that all of your tires are below the recommended level, you lose 1% on your gas mileage. Most car tires are five to ten PSI below the normal level, so that means by just airing up your tires, you can improve your gas mileage by up to 5%. It's basically free gas!

37. Start a garden. Gardening is an inexpensive hobby that supplements your grocery bill (depending on your water usage).

38. Engage in your community. There are often tons of free events going on in your town that you don't even know about. Stop by the local library or by city hall and ask how you can get ahold of a listing of upcoming community events, and make an effort to hit the interesting ones. You can often get free meals, free entertainment, and free stuff just by paying attention .

39. Pack food before you go on a road trip. Have everyone pack a sack lunch for the trip. That way, instead of stopping in the middle of the trip, driving around looking for a place to eat, spending a bunch of time there, and then paying a hefty bill, you can just eat on the road or, better yet, stop at a nice park and stretch for a bit. Plus, you'll save a lot of money and time this way.

40. Use a simple razor to shave. The 99¢ and Dollar Stores have some of the best razors I've ever tried…and they actually last longer than the $10 razors. Try several types and stores for the razor that works best for you. $9 savings per razor package is significant savings especially if you use a new razor once a week or twice a month.

41. Start a free hobby like Reading or Hiking. Reading is one of the cheapest – and most beneficial – hobbies around. Most towns have a library available to the public – just go there and check out some books that interest you. Then, spend some of your free time in a cozy place in your house, just reading away. You'll learn something new, improve your reading ability, enjoy yourself, and not have to

spend a dime. If you are a more active type, pick up running, hiking, pick up games or volleyball at the park. Join a meet up with similar interests you have…they have free activities for dancers to dog lovers.

42. Always ask for fees to be waived. Any time you sign up for a service of any kind and there are sign-up fees, ask for them to be waived. Sometimes (but not always), they will be.

43. Don't overspend on hygiene products. Shop generic, make your own, or buy only when on sale.

44. Eat less meat. For the nutritional value, meat is very expensive, especially as compared to vegetables and fruits. Try to plan your meals with "meat as an accent flavor" rather than being the main event. For example, remember that salad bar in your fridge tip? Take chicken and bacon bits as the accent flavors to your salad which is the main dish vs. a side salad next to bacon wrapped chicken breast. Try to use the 80/20 rule – 20% meat.

45. Use coupons. Use coupons only for what you regularly buy or need. Don't buy unless you actually use it.

46. Make your own beer or wine. If you enjoy an occasional drink, this is a great way to enjoy some of the beverages that you love at a very cheap price, and it starts a new hobby that will keep you away from boredom shopping.

47. Are you a FOMO spender? Host a BYOBW event at home. Everyone brings their favorite bottle of wine or six pack and an appetizer. For the price of one glass of wine or two beers, you can buy a bottle or a six pack. For those of you that suffer from FOMO (fear of missing out), the trick to saving money is to become the person that everyone else experiences FOMO because your house is where everyone wants to hang.

48. Cut down on your vacation spending. Instead of going on a big, extravagant trip, pack up the car and see some of America some years for vacation.

49. Exercise more. Go for a walk or a jog each evening, and practice stretching and some light muscle

exercise at home. These exercises can be done at home for very little, meaning you've got an activity without a lot of cost, and the health benefits are enormous. Just set aside some time each day to get some exercise, and your body and wallet will thank you.

50. Buy in bulk. Buy items you use a lot of in bulk, particularly items that don't perish – trash bags, laundry detergent, diapers, and so on are purchased in the largest amounts possible. Although, price check before you buy. Bulk is not always cheaper.

51. Don't beat yourself up when you make a mistake. Even if you make ten good choices, it's easy to beat yourself up and feel like a failure over one bad choice. If you make a big mistake and realize it, and try to apply that later on. Use the motto, "Fail Forward".

52. Don't buy designer labels. If you must have a designer name on your body, shop consignment and thrift stores. Yes, there are designer labels at thrift stores. ShopGoodwill.com offers Coach, Louis Vuitton, Gucci, and a ton more designers on online auction and you can snag something at the fraction of retail. I bought a Juicy Couture book bag for $7 and a Brighton bucket purse for $10. I bought Ferragamo sandals at Savers for $10...fou nd them online for $140 retail.

53. Book flights early, and book them with a carrier that will allow you to change or cancel without charging you fees.

54. Shop alone. Children, friends who love shopping, or even just a friend whose tastes you respect can influence you to spend extra money.[8]

55. Pay in full and in cash. Credit and debit cards increase spending for two reasons: you have much more money available to spend than you normally would, and because no visible money is changing hands, it doesn't register as a "real" purchase.

56. Don't be fooled by marketing. Outside influences are a huge factor affecting what we spend our money

on. Be vigilant and try to be aware of all the reasons you're drawn to a product.

57. Don't purchase something just because it's reduced price.] Coupons and sales are great for products you were already planning to buy; purchasing something you don't need just because it's 50% off does not save money.

58. Round Up. Be aware of pricing tricks. Translate that "$1.99" price into "$2". Judge the price of an item on its own merits, not because it's a "better deal" than another option by the same company.

59. Take all the costs into account. You'll end up paying a lot more than the sticker price for many big-ticket items. Read all the fine print and add up the total amount before making your decision. If you are using a charge card and making interest payments, then add $1000 to any purchase you make with your card because it will most likely take you 1-5 years to pay that item off. Therefore, your $100 sweater…is it really worth $1100? Because in the end, that is what you are likely to pay. It takes approximately 88 years to pay off $1000 by paying the minimum $10.00/month. In reality a $1000 purchase will turn into $10 560 at the end of those 88 years. Is it really a bargain at that point?

60. Do I have something that serves the same purpose? People have kitchens full of specialized products and many of the multipurpose products in your home can perform the same task a specialized product can.

61. Simple buy less food. If you always buy a pound of lunch meat, buy 3/4. Buy a dozen eggs instead of 18.

62. Ditch soda and soft drinks. Drink water. Tap water is fine or buy a Brita, not bottled water.

63. Ditch bottled water, you don't need it. Stop buying bottled water! A case of bottled water is about $5 per week, $20 a month and $240 a year! Try a refillable bottle instead… Brita makes a refillable bottle with a filter.

64. If you don't want to clip coupons, at least get your grocery store loyalty card if it gets your discounts.

65. Before going to a restaurant, do an internet search to see if you can find coupons or a "kids eat free" night, or a discounted gift card at restaurant.com.

66. If spending is out of control, cut up credit cards. Go to a cash only system with envelopes and leave everything else at home.

67. Get online magazine subscriptions for Kindles instead of paper, or get truly free magazine subscriptions.

68. Always search for a discount, promo, or coupon code before you buy online.

69. Join a Facebook group to buy and sell things. Search "your town" and yard sale to see what comes up. Find items cheaper and make some money on things you're no longer using.

70. Cut back on what activities your kids do. Unstructured play time has lots of value.

71. Get in the habit of saying "Is that the best price? Are there any discounts available?" You will be surprised!

72. Pay your kids to wash your car and cut your grass instead of a more expensive service. Or, wash your car yourself.

73. Try to give up paper towels and other disposable cleaning items and buy stuff built to last.

74. Always try a free version of an app or website before purchasing it's paid version.

75. Keep a list in your purse of every gift giving occasion that you have in a year. Every holiday, birthdays, teacher gifts, etc. Then, if you run into a great sale or clearance, get out your list and see what you need to get. Maintain a gift closet of great deal finds that you find and save money on gift giving.

76. See if it is worth it for you to buy coupons for your favorite products (only) from a clipping service. Specifically for 'free product' coupons so to stock up on all the laundry, cleaning, toiletries., and other things that last and can be stored for long periods of time.

77. Make your own 'specialty' foods at home rather than plopping down $5 for each jar of fancy condiment at the market.

78. The stores and credit companies can't track your purchases if you use cash. Your identity and credit card numbers can't be stolen when you use cash too.

79. Make going out to eat a once a week or so treat, and the rest of the time cook at home.

80. Build in a staple meal or two that is easy to prepare on a day when food plans fall through, or your too exhausted to cook much.

81. Beware of luxuries dressed up as necessities. If your income doesn't cover your costs, then some of your spending is probably for luxuries - even if you've been considering them to be filling a real need.

82. The most common spending problems are caused by a house that's too large, a car that's too luxurious or a credit-card lifestyle that's too lavish for your income. Simplify. Simplify. Simplify.

83. Shop only with discounted gift cards for places you normally shop. . Buy discounted gift cards for up to 30% off at Cardpool.com or Giftcards.com

84. Make sure you're taking advantage of discounts! Military, Student, or Teacher Discounts.

85. Carry a spending tracker with you everywhere you go. Write down everything to the penny.

86. Try swapping instead of shopping. Invite your friends over and swap children's clothes, toys, books and Halloween costumes. The average family saves $569 a year by swapping children's clothes!

87. Use The Grocery Game, Inc.to maximize your savings. The Grocery Game helps you combine coupons with sales for huge savings and even a few free items each week. You will save at least $50 a week, and you can get started with a free trial!

88. Off hours shopping. Did you know that Kroger sells rotisserie chickens for half price after 7:30? Stock up, chop up, freeze!. Meijer sells all pre-sliced deli lunchmeat for half price after 8:30. See if your local grocery has a similar policy. Check your local bagel and donut shops, you can likely pick up a bargain after a certain time of the day! Our bagel shop sells 1 dozen for $5 after 2:00, and I've heard that Krispy

Kreme sells a dozen donuts (the ones in the case) for $1 after midnight...that gives new meaning to a midnight snack!

89. Bring back home birthday parties! Do you really need to spend more than $50 for a 1-year old's birthday party? A rule of thumb can be to increase the birthday party budget by $10 for every year of your child's birthday. Start with $50 and add $10 each year. Make it a family policy. That way by the time your child is 13 (a very critical social age) you child can choose...does she want a party for $170 or does she want to pocket some of that?

90. Hyper- mile- ing. Hybermileing. Slow acceleration saves a ton of gas, as well as letting the weight of your car take you to red lights, etc. My van has a miles per gallon currently setting. I tried this and watched it go from 11.5 to 13.7 miles to the gallon. I have learned how to get an extra 2.2 miles to the gallon when I drive that thing. I usually drive my more effective car but to watch it, I tested this in the van with a meter to watch my savings. I apply this in all my cars. I have heard that you can Google search hypermileing on Google and find out more. (I must add I live in a FLAT part of the country)

91. Dumpster diving. This is a personal choice. Check out privately owned stores. Talk to them and see if you can get their produce out the front door witch is set for the dumpster, if not get it out of the dumpster. I have save so much money doing this. Things like bags of oranges are amazing. One bad orange get's the bag thrown out! Throw the bad one out and eat the rest. Clean everything. Never get into a dumpster though.

92. Kroger's offers gas discounts based on purchases. Buy gift cards for other stores at Kroger's (like Lowe's, Home Depot, Applebees). You can 10 cents to $2 a gallon on fuel at Kroger's.

93. If you like to buy organic and natural, you should try looking into a local food co-op where you buy in bulk at the cost to the store. Sometimes people in the co-op will split cases of products and you still

get the savings without having too much of something you can't finish.

94. Look into buying farm fresh eggs. You can get organic free range farm fresh eggs, (sometimes delivered!) for half the price you'll find them at your grocery store.

95. Use plants as gifts. You can grow your own and share, or you can often find them on craigslist for free.

96. Use fresh fruit and veggie basket as a gift. Buy baskets at a thrift shop for 50 cents to $2, the fill it with fresh produce from your own garden or from a local gardener or orchard for a big discount.

97. Only drink water at restaurants. Water is free and if you have a family of 5 that could be $10 just for drinks! If you go out 2 times a week that's $20 a week $80 a month and $1,040 a year!

98. Look to buy Christmas gifts (usually toys) during holiday sales such as 4th of July.

99. Target and other stores may allow coupon stacking. Go through their ads to see what is on sale and look for both a target and a manufacturer coupon shopping.

100. Check your credit score before you go shopping…especially for big ticket items. If you have a lower credit score, you will pay as much as 10% more in annual interest rate. This difference can equal tens of thousands of dollars. Credit.com gives ideas on what kind of credit you need to increase your score. Credikarma.com also gives you simulations of what a credit or purchasing move will do to your credit score. If you can wait six months to purchase the item, then take that six months to improve your credit score, then buy the big ticket item.

Saving Your Money

Saving:

Strategies & Concepts

Savings Basics

Excerpt from the Women's Money® Guidebook –
for the full chapter, join the Women's Money Mentoring program.

Saving money isn't always easy, but sometimes getting started is the main roadblock. Many people feel like there just isn't "enough money" to pay bills, let alone think about saving money for the future. Having savings helps to build financial security. Without money set aside for the future, it will be difficult to meet future emergencies; pay large and infrequent bills; or to build resources for important longer-term goals, like a car, a home, a college education, or retirement.

This will help you learn:

> 1) Why paying yourself first is an important strategy.
> 2) How to establish an emergency fund and a set-aside account.
> 3) How to select savings options that make sense for you.

As you read about investing, you are certain to come across words and concepts that are unfamiliar to you. Check the Women's Money Glossary for an explanation. A helpful on-line reference is www. Investorwords.com. Write down words you plan to look up.

Why You Should Pay Yourself First

The golden rule of savings is to pay yourself first. By adding to your savings regularly, you will gain control of your financial life. By setting aside money before you can spend it, you may not even miss it! Many people say they will start saving after they have paid all of their bills. They are missing the mark! There will always be ways to spend money! It takes less discipline to pay yourself first than to hunt for ways to save money after the bills are paid.

As soon as you receive your paycheck, make it a habit to pay yourself first. You can even make saving money effortless by automating your savings; have savings automatically drafted from your checking account each month- that way you will not have to think about it. Taking the step to pay yourself first will build a sense of accomplishment and satisfaction when you see your savings account balance grow.

Keep Your Financial Goals in Mind

List your top three financial goals. (If you have completed the goal-setting exercises from previous chapters of this handbook, just copy your top three financial goals here. If this chapter is your starting point, list your three most important financial goals here. Your financial goals provide a roadmap for the future.

First Stop: Emergency Savings

Despite signs that Americans are starting to adopt a new frugality as measured by a rise in the personal savings rate as a share of disposable income, half of U.S. households don't have even modest savings, according to a new study conducted by TNS Group, a market researcher, along with Harvard Business School and Dartmouth College professors. The researchers surveyed households to see how many could come up with $2,000 in 30 days to cope with an emergency like a car breakdown or major home repair. About half said they could not come up with $2,000 for a "rainy day" even if they turned to relatives for help. Researchers pointed to a tougher credit environment that has made it more difficult for consumers to rely on credit for emergencies, thus causing households to live with what one of the researchers calls "financial fragility."

Life is unpredictable. Having an emergency fund is the best way to weather financial storms and uncertainty. Most financial advisers recommend that we have emergency savings equivalent of three to six months' worth of living expenses. However, some experts recommend a fund large enough to cover eight or nine months' living expenses.

How should we go about creating this fund for emergencies? Here are some practical ideas for creating your own emergency fund.

We should note here that unlike any other financial education program, Women's Money advocates for two emergency savings funds. Even though we encourage two funds, please know that you have to do what works best for you and your life. How you get there is not as important as getting and staying there.

Why Create Two Emergency Funds?

Real Life, Real Money: Tanisha Learns a Hard Lesson

Tanisha is 28 and a single mom of Angelina, who is two. Tanisha works as an executive assistant for a casino executive. One day at work, she gets a call that from her daughter's day care that Angelina had a severe head injury on the playground and has been taken to the hospital. Tanisha hangs up, tells her boss of the situation and heads to the hospital. Luckily, Tanisha has good insurance and her emergency savings has three months salary in it, so she can pay for the hospital co-pay, so Tanisha is no worried about the money. She can focus completely on her daughter who was placed in ICU.

Tanisha's daughter is doing well, and will be able to leave ICU shortly. Tanisha's mother holds watch over Angelina, so Tanisha can go back to work the next day. Tanisha didn't even miss a full day of work. She was back to work the next day. Unfortunately, when she returned to work she was fired because she told her boss she was leaving and didn't ask for permission to leave.

When Tanisha sat down to do the numbers, she realized that the hospital co-pay ate up one-third of her emergency savings and now she was left with only two months of living expenses. Her daughter's condition and finding a new job was stressful enough, but now she had once less month to do it in.

Tanisha thought she was prepared, but it turns out she wasn't prepared properly.

First Stop: Create an Emergency Fund

1.   Start by looking at your life, family and work. What are some of the possible emergencies that could happen?

       a.   Do you have a parent or children across country? You have to be prepared with airfare, hotel and spending money in case you need to fly out for a family emergency.

       b.   Do you have a car? Cars break down. If you have an expensive car, your emergency fund may have to be higher than if you had a basic American made car.

       c.   Do you have animals?   Plan for their potential emergencies.

       d.   Do you live in an area where weather-related disasters like a hurricane or flood are likely to occur?

       e.   Do you have a home warranty?   Research the maximum you would have to pay for the worst covered expense. If you don't have a home warranty, plan to save the price of a washing machine or more. If you don't have a credit card, then estimate the price of a new furnace or water heater.

       f. What else might be an emergency you would have to pay for in your life?

2.   Calculate the costs of your possible emergencies.

3.   Choose the emergency situation that would cost you the most as the minimum amount you want to have in your emergency fund. Only you can decide what your emergency fund goal should be.

4.   Designate a special savings account as your emergency fund. Although current interest rates are low, select an account that will accrue interest or earnings and offers liquidity so you can withdraw funds when an emergency occurs. However, don't make it SO EASY that you will "raid" the fund every time you need a little "extra." That defeats the purpose of having an emergency fund. Look at your emergency fund as your "peace of mind fund." By having funds available to cover future emergencies, you are building a cushion to fall back on should some unforeseen, serious financial emergency occur in your life.

5.   Decide how long it will take you to build up your emergency fund. It will take time to build up your emergency fund because you are funding it from your current income. Your current income has many demands on it, including current bills that are due. If you have another source of funds, you can make faster progress in building up your emergency fund. Perhaps you can use a pay raise, a bonus, income from interest or dividends, or a source of income other than your pay to start or increase your emergency fund. If you pay off a debt that you've been paying towards every month, perhaps you can use the money you would have used for the debt to fund or increase your emergency fund. If you receive a tax refund, you could add money from it to your emergency fund.

Second Stop: Create a Pink-Slip Fund™

1.   Start by doing the math. What are your "bare bones" living expenses each month? How does this figure compare to what you actually spend right now? A Pink-Slip Fund™ is intended to cover your basic living expenses should you experience losing your source of income. Another way to think about a Pink-Slip Fund™ is to ask yourself the question, "What is the least amount of money I would need to cover the basics and not fall behind with my bills?" In times of emergency, that probably means doing away with spending for non-essentials. We're talking survival here!

2.   Once you know the "bare bones" amount for one month's living expenses, multiply that amount by the number of months you want your Pink-Slip Fund™ to ultimately cover. Should it be three, six, eight, or more months? Only you can decide what your emergency fund goal should be.

3.   Decide how long it will take you to build up your Pink-Slip Fund™. Remember that Rome was not built in a day, and you cannot fully fund your Pink-Slip Fund™ overnight! Take your time, and be realistic about it. It will take time to build up your emergency fund because you are funding it from your current income. Your current income has many demands on it, including current bills that are due. If you have another source of funds, you can make faster progress in building up your Pink-Slip Fund™. Perhaps you can use a pay raise, a bonus, income from interest or dividends, or a source of income other than your pay to start or increase your Pink-Slip Fund™. If you pay off a debt that you've

been paying towards every month, perhaps you can use the money you would have used for the debt to fund or increase your emergency fund. If you receive a tax refund, you could add money from it to your Pink-Slip Fund™.

4.   Determine if you already have a fund from your employer that can act as a Pink-Slip Fund™. Do you have employee benefits that you can cash out like accrued sick leave or vacation days you never took? Talk to your employer to see what you may have available to you without penalty of early withdrawal.

5.   Designate a special savings account as your Pink-Slip Fund™. Although current interest rates are low, select an account that will accrue interest or earnings and offers liquidity so you can withdraw funds when an emergency occurs. However, don't make it SO EASY that you will "raid" the fund every time you need a little "extra." That defeats the purpose of having an emergency fund. Look at your Pink-Slip Fund™ as your "take a breath fund." By having funds available to cover loss of income, you can take a breath and find the best income replacement and even create a plan to replace that income rather than jumping at the first job offer that comes along.

Third Stop: Set-Aside Accounts

You may be unfamiliar with "set- aside accounts" since not all financial advice books or advisors refer to these special accounts. They aren't quite the same as an emergency fund. Emergency funds are not meant to be tapped regularly, while set-aside accounts are meant to be tapped regularly.
So, what is the point of a set-aside account, you might ask?

It's a place to put money that you know you will need in the future, instead of just keeping it in your primary checking account where using it for other purposes is too easy. Another way of looking at the difference between an emergency fund and a set-aside account is that emergency funds are to be used for sudden, unexpected events; set-aside accounts are for known expenses that occur periodically. A bill for your annual umbrella insurance premium is not an emergency; it is a known occurrence. Of course, if you don't have the money to pay the bill, it is very, very stressful. The following two cases should illustrate two ways in which set-aside accounts can be used, for expenses and for income.

Set Aside Accounts Can Work for Regular Expenses Too

Do you find that you take money from your budget to pay for unexpected extras? For instance, do you overspend on groceries or shopping and then take it from that extra money you were planning to put towards your credit card pay off? This is not uncommon. Being out in the world is pretty tempting, and we don't have an angel on our shoulder reminding us that if we splurge now, we have to take it from somewhere else later. Therefore some people have set-aside "accounts" for regular budgeted expenses too. There are many ways to format these. You have to work this in a way that works for YOU. Try several methods to see what works for you.

Multiple Ways to Create a Regular Expense Set-Aside System

1.   The envelope system. This is a tried and true system around for many years that has been very successful for many people. How does it work? Get a bunch of envelopes and label them to correspond with each spending category in your budget. Cash your check and put in the budgeted amount in that envelope. Put the envelopes in a safe place. That's what you have to spend in that c category, and because you have cash, you can't go over budget.

2.   The debit card system. This one is a little tricky, but if you don't feel comfortable with cash and envelopes, this is the same concept but a checking account acts as your "envelope". You open up a free checking account per budget category and have a debit card related to that account. You can only spend what you have in your account. This is also a good way to protect your money from identity theft as only a small part of your money could be at risk rather than your whole paycheck in your main account.

3.   Flexible vs. Fixed system. This method is a bit easier to manage than multiple debit cards and checking accounts. Your budget is already divided into fixed and flexible expenses, so you can have two accounts. The fixed expenses account is never touched. Every bill is on auto-pay (rent, car, insurance, etc). The

second account is for flexible expenses such as groceries, clothing, gas, etc. You can also split the flexible spending into two accounts one for essentials like groceries and gas and one for fun money like clothing and eating out.

4. Per Pay-Check system. Determine which bills you will pay out of each paycheck. Put it in writing. When the paycheck comes in, pay the bills and pay your savings account. Use the remainder for flexible expenses.

Do You Need Separate Savings Accounts for Your Emergency Fund and Your Set-Aside Accounts?

No? Maybe? Yes?

The answer is "yes" if it is easier for you to maintain separate accounts. The answer is "no" if your long-term strategy is to use a single account as a "holding tank" for money you plan to accumulate in the account and periodically transfer funds to pay for set-asides or for emergencies. It may be less costly to have a single account because it is easier to meet minimum balance requirements. You may also prefer receiving a single statement with all of your transactions. Within a single account, track your sub- account balances. This is easy if you use a computerized financial recordkeeping system.

Comparing Savings Options

Where to Put Your Money Not only must you decide what type of savings option to select, you must be able to compare choices within those options. For example, savings accounts appear to be alike when they advertise an identical Annual Percentage Rate (APR), but research has shown that there can be big differences in earnings because of the numerous ways in which earnings can be calculated. The Truth-in- Savings law requires all financial institutions to disclose the terms and conditions of savings plans. Some general questions to ask before making a decision about any savings plan include:

1. How safe is money in this particular institution and savings plan? Is it insured?

2. Is the financial institution on- line (on the Internet), in my community, or both?

3. Are there minimum balance requirements?

4. Are there penalties and fees for transactions?

5. How convenient is it to make deposits and withdrawals?

6. What is the Annual Percentage Rate?

7. What is the Annual Percentage Yield (APY)?

8. How often is interest compounded?

9. What method is used to compute interest?

10. What special features or services are offered?

11. Are there any tax advantages or disadvantages associated with this savings instrument?

12. Does the account offer Internet- based electronic transfers? How long will it take before amounts that are transferred become available to me?

13. Can the account be accessed and managed on-line?

Don't Do the 52-Week Money Challenge
(At Least Not Their Way)
by Carrie Rocha

Have you seen the 52-Week Money Challenge all over social media since New Year's Day? I have. I'm not a fan. You're challenged to save $1,378 this year by:

Saving increasing amounts each week. Start with $1 during week one. Then, increase your savings by $1 each subsequent week. That means in week 37 you save $37 and on week 52 you sock away $52.

Putting the money in a jar. You paste a savings chart to a jar, then put it on your kitchen counter so you'll never forget to put a week's savings in it. (Seriously, Pinterest is home to thousands of these cutesy money-filled jar photos. Don't search it. I dare you not to.)

Don't Do It! (That Way)
Look, I'm all for saving money. Over the next 52 weeks I'm even aiming to save $1,378, just like those in the 52-Week Money Challenge. But, I'm not doing the 52-Week Money Challenge as I've seen it presented. I'm doing it PYD (Pocket Your Dollars) Style.

Here's what I am going to do instead (and, I'd really super duper love to have you do this too):

Save a Decreasing Amount Each Week

This week I'm going to set aside $52. Then next week, I'm going to decrease the amount I save by a buck and set aside $51. On week 37 I'll save $16 and on week 52 I'll save a whopping $1.

Why?

Immediate results. After four weeks I'll have an extra $202 in the bank. Under the rules of their challenge you would have saved a measly $10. In fact, it'd take you until week 20 to save $200+

under their system. After 4 weeks of doing this the PYD way, you'll have something real and valuable to show for your efforts. Don't believe me that immediate results matter? Which 4-week weight loss plan would intrigue you more – one that yields a 1 pound drop or a 12 pound drop? Immediate results motivate.

Get the heavy lifting done. If $202 seems like a lot of money to save in January, then trust me, it'd be an impossible amount for you in December (sorry if the truth hurts). Let's do the hard work right now, when our motivation is highest. Then, come next Christmastime we only need to find an extra $10 in our budget. Nice.

Get Your Money Off the Kitchen Counter

Instead of saving money in a jar, I'm going to save it in my free Capital One 360 savings account. Why?

We consume things in jars. Jars are for jelly. And pickles. And mayonnaise. Consumable products come in jars. This challenge is about saving. It's not about consuming, so a jar is the wrong tool. If you like the visual impact of watching a savings jar fill up, then use our 52-week money challenge printable chart to track your progress.

Distance is good. My financial life changed, for the better, when I distanced myself from my savings (I say lots more about that in my book). I know myself. If I had a jar of money sitting on my kitchen counter, then I'd order pizza. Or, I'd get treats from the ice cream truck or an occasional Starbucks. I want to ensure that I will have $1,378 at year's end (nothing spent out of it). To make that happen, I'll automate deposits into my free Capital One 360 savings account. (The icing on the cake of these Capital One accounts is that it takes 3 days for money to transfer back into your main checking account, which means it's impossible to use the funds to cover a potentially bounced check.)

52-Week Money Challenge PYD Style

I'm raring to go with this year-long challenge. Are you with me? Here's how we'll do this:

Decide. Commit yourself to the cause. Are you willing to do what it takes to save $1,378 over the next year? If you are, then decide what you are saving for. I'd recommend you save toward an emergency fund, unless you already have 3 months of living expenses set aside. Personally, we have an emergency fund so I'm earmarking this money toward my family's $2,000 medical deductible (I like to have that money saved, on hand, just in case – God forbid we need it).

Open a free Capital One 360 savings account. If you don't already have a free Capital One 360 savings account earmarked for your purpose, then open one. My family has multiple Capital One 360 accounts, with the oldest one being 12 years old. (Note: your credit will not be pulled when you apply for a savings account.) (Full disclosure: I do earn a referral bonus if you open an account via my link, but I LOVED them for y-e-a-r-s before I knew about that. I'd recommend them if they didn't offer that.)
Set up your January transfers. Pick the day each week you want transfers to happen (Friday, perhaps?), then set up your first four transfers*:

- Week 1: $52
- Week 2: $51
- Week 3: $50
- Week 4: $49

*If $200 seems like an overwhelming amount for you to save right now, then find a lesser number that still stretches you. Think – what can you sell? What services can you offer others (babysitting, pet sitting, walk the dog, shovel sidewalks, etc.)? What can you go without for a few months so you have money to save?
Track your progress. Use this free 52-week money challenge printable chart to track your progress. (A huge thanks to the talented Jen Goode of 100Directions.com for creating that chart for us).

What do you think? Are you going to do this year-long challenge PYD style? What are you doing to make $202 available for you to save this month?

Importance of Credit in Saving Money
By Julie Macc excerpted from
DIY Credit Restoration: 10-step guide to a better credit life

Credit ratings/reports impact nearly every facet of your life. If you have ever been denied a loan or even a job due to your credit, then you already know the importance your credit profile has to your life.

The quality of your credit affects your monthly living expenses. Home loans, rent, car payments, credit cards, installment loans, car insurance, cell phone plans, health and life insurance, and even utility deposit can be impacted by the quality of your credit rating. Credit ratings may determine where you live, and even where you work. Do you rent or own your dream home? The answer may be based on credit factors. Some employers rely on credit reports to help make hiring decisions.1 Today, trying to hide your credit history rarely works.

But you can take control of your credit profile and make sure it presents the most accurate picture possible.

The scary truth: Most consumers don't know how credit works or even what that magical credit score really means. This book demystifies your credit profile for you. And, as you already know, there is a dramatic difference in quality of life for those with bad credit vs. those with good credit.

Life with Bad Credit

You can live with poor credit. But every year those credit issues will cost you thousands and thousands of dollars extra. That makes it harder just to survive, and nearly impossible to save money for the future.

This is one of the fundamental reasons the United States savings rate has stayed under 4% overall – and below 1% for many sectors. Many consumers don't have the extra money to save because they are paying thousands and thousands of dollars each year in outlandish interest charges.

Having worked for consumer credit law firms since 2002, I have reviewed thousands of credit reports with clients to find inaccurate reporting. Most of my clients had no idea how much their credit was really costing them every day – or how correcting wrong information would save them thousands of dollars and improve their lives.

Many knew that their bad credit made it hard to get approved for new credit. But in reality, my clients, like most consumers, never REALLY knew how much credit impacts their day-to-day lives.

Bad credit ruins lives. Credit quality can be the difference between living life in financial comfort and struggling just to survive.

Let's look at a car as a simple example. Most Americans rely on cars to get around. We drive to get to our jobs, to take our kids to day care, or just to get to the store. There are an estimated 250 million car owners in the U.S. alone, so chances are pretty good you, or someone you know, owns a car.

Most of us take out loans to buy a car. We pay it back in monthly payments until the debt is paid off. The interest rate we pay on that car loan (and most other loans) is based on our credit history and our credit scores.

The lender will use those factors to decide on an interest rate based on the consumer's ability to pay back that loan. The payments will then be established based on the loan amount, interest rate, and term of the loan.

With good credit, you will get approved for a longer term and better interest rate. With bad credit, you will pay much greater interest on a shorter term, making your payments much higher.

Okay, so maybe you already knew all that. Many consumers do, but most don't know how much that extra interest and shorter terms really costs them.

A car dealer may offer a person with good credit a loan on a new car with a 0 to 5% interest rate. That same dealer would either refuse to finance a loan to a person with poor credit or offer them a much higher interest rate.

The result: The person with bad credit would have a higher monthly payment. Paying just $100 a month more on that loan will cost $1,200 more a year – or $6,000 more over a five year loan.

This example is not extreme. Many people with poor credit end up with much higher payments for everything they buy.

Rent and home expenses are another area where customers with poor credit are forced to pay extra amounts of interest. In 2015, good credit borrowers could qualify for 30-year home mortgages with interest rates well under 4%. Borrowers with poor credit would not qualify for those great rates. So just like with car loans, every $100 more per month that they pay amounts to thousands and thousands of dollars over the life of the loan.

In addition, mortgage lenders require consumers with credit scores of 620 or lower to pay Private Mortgage Insurance (PMI) when getting a mortgage. PMI typically adds several hundred dollars a month to the borrower's monthly payment.

Most people know credit has an adverse effect on their life. But the truth is, bad credit controls their lives. They pay outrageous amounts of extra interest charges each and every month. That debt and those higher payments strap individuals and families, forcing them to live paycheck-to-paycheck.

Bad credit also impacts children. If a student's family has poor credit and his or her parents have not saved for college, that student may not qualify for a student loan.

If even one emergency arises, many consumers with poor credit are susceptible to a total financial catastrophe. With bad credit, their lives are just like a house of cards waiting to collapse.

Consumers with credit issues don't have credit cards with high borrowing limits to use in case of emergencies. If their car's transmission goes out or their child needs emergency dental treatment, their only options may be pay day loans. The rates on these types of loans are extremely high (some charge 100% a month), making them almost impossible to pay off.

Life is tough with bad credit, really tough. With no available credit, one emergency can wipe you out. And all the money paid in extra interest each month means most can't build up a savings account or an emergency fund. Many people are so caught up with financial survival, they forget about how innocently it all began. Instead, they are caught in a trap that few can actually escape.

Saving: Tools

- Mint: Securely consolidate your accounts, track how much money you're spending and receive alerts when bills are due. You can also set reminders and personal finance goals, tag expenditures by category, and view your financial data as simple charts or Excel spreadsheets. This little powerhouse allows you to keep track of all your financial activity from all your accounts: checking, savings, retirement—you name it! Every transaction is automatically recorded and categorized. Mint makes note of your spending patterns and creates a budget. Additionally, on the iPad, it generates graphs to give you visual representations of your net worth and cash flow. For those worried about security, the app is password protected and there is a way to deactivate access from your phone through the Mint website. It is a fantastic way to keep tabs on your overall financial health and be able to spot potential problems. FREE. Available for: iOS and Android

- Walmart Savings Catcher: Enter or scan your receipt. Enter your receipt number or scan the barcode by downloading the Walmart App. App compare prices. Walmart will match the price of any local competitor's printed ad for an identical product. You get the difference. If Savings Catcher finds a lower advertised price, you get the difference. FREE.

- BillTracker: Passcode-protected BillTracker allows you to keep all due dates and amount totals in one place and even gives you notifications for impending payments. Due dates are highlighted on the calendar for quick views. Available for: iOS

- You Need a Budget (YNAB): The name says it all: YNAB is an incredibly detailed but easy-to-use budget interface. The software operates by four simple rules: 1) Give every dollar a job, 2) Save for a rainy day, 3) Roll with the punches, and 4) Live on last month's income. YNAB's goal is to change the way you manage money and to create stress-free finances. The app is supplemental to the $60 software you purchase for your Windows or Mac and is meant to allow users to check their transactions and budgetary restrictions on-the-go. Available for: iOS and Android

- Shopkick: Browse products, find inspiration, and discover great deals at stores like Target, Macy's, Best Buy, and more. Users are able to earn points by making purchases, inviting friends to join, and even by just walking into the stores. Then, the points can be transformed into gift cards at partnering stores. Available for: iOS and Android

- Ibotta: Ibotta allows shoppers to earn real money for shopping. Start by perusing the different offers in the product gallery and choose the ones you're interested in. Every time you compete a "task" (like sharing on Facebook, taking a poll, or watching a video), pending cash is added to your account that can be accessed once you actually purchase the product from one of the 50 retailers partnered with Ibotta. Once the purchase is verified, cash is put into your PayPal account or turned into gift cards. Available for: iOS and Android

- RetailMeNot: "Thousands of coupons in your pocket." Browse coupons and deals from hundreds of retailers. Save the coupons you want to use for easy access and get notifications for coupon expiration dates. You can also search for deals at the nearest stores. Don't worry about printing the coupons; all you have to do is show your phone at the register. Available for: iOS and Android

- SnipSnap: Like RetailMeNot, however, this one also lets you take pictures of printed coupons from many retailers and turns them into digital, mobile-ready ones. You can also browse the online directory and see the coupons that friends have "snipped." Available for: iOS

- Grocery iQ: Stay on task and avoid impulse purchases with this incredibly detailed grocery shopping list platform. Not only can you build grocery lists by searching through the millions of products in the app's database, but you can use voice recognition or barcode scanning. Grocery iQ also has a store locator feature and offers coupons. This app is a must-have for busy families or for anyone trying to keep their grocery budget under control. Available for: iOS and Android

- SavingStar: SavingStar is a digital coupon app for thousands of grocery stores and drugstores that is linked to your individual store loyalty cards. (you have to have loyalty cards to get rewards.) You choose the digital coupons you want to use and the reward is applied to your loyalty card and when you reach $5 in savings, you earn cash! You can even opt for your cash savings to go towards donations for the charity American Forests.Available for: iOS and Android

- Groupon: Redeem Groupon deals (as much as 50-90% off!) on everything from restaurants to retailers to hotels. You can search by location to find deals closest to you. Available for: iOS, Android, and Windows

- LivingSocial: Similar to Groupon, you can use this app to gain hand-held access to all of LivingSocial's deals.. An added bonus: if you share a discount you received on your social media accounts and three of your friends purchase the same deal, you'll get yours free of charge! Available for: iOS, Android, and Windows

- Amazon Local: "Save up to 75% in your city." Use this app to find Amazon-level deals on the go. What's great about Amazon Local is that you can search for deals and buy them instantly right from your phone. Like the other discount apps mentioned, there is no need to print out coupons or vouchers. Available for: iOS, Android, and Kindle Fire

- Scoutmob: An exceptionally clever app. In addition to finding great discounts at different eateries and shops, you can also search through articles and other local happenings. Available for: iOS and Android

- DebtTracker Pro: For those working their way out of debt, DebtTracker Pro can serve as a payoff plan and can help you keep track of your road to financial recovery. Users are able to choose their strategy for overcoming debt and the app not only recommends payment strategies but sends reminders when payments are due. There is a visual reminder of how close you are to your goal (sorted by account) to serve as further incentive. Getting out of debt is a long and difficult process, but this app will help keep you organized. Available for: iOS

- Viggle: An app that awards you for watching TV?! Viggle lets users "check in" to whatever show they're watching and earn points to be redeemed for rewards from Starbucks, Barnes & Noble, and other great brands. You can earn additional points by testing your television IQ and playing games. The app also allows you to interact with friends. Available for: iOS and Android

- Military Cost Cutters: This app is a must-have for military personnel and their families. This free application allows veterans to find military-friendly businesses in their area that offer discounts for their service. You are able to search by city, state, and zip code for best results. Available for: iOS and Android

- GasBuddy: Gas prices can be a major headache, but with GasBuddy, you can find the cheapest gas prices closest to you! Additionally, for every gas price you report, you earn points towards winning the weekly $250 prize for gas. With over 32 million visitors, the app remains extraordinarily up-to-date on your best gas deals. Available for: iOS, Android, Blackberry and Windows

- Hotel Tonight: This international app allows you to find incredibly low prices on last-minute hotel bookings. Amazingly, you can arrange same-day bookings until 2 a.m. and for multiple nights. This service is a lifesaver for everything from unexpected layovers to spontaneous vacations. Hotel Tonight is constantly adding new locations and has stellar 24/7 customer support to keep their customers happy.Available for: iOS and Android

- BestParking: Trying to find affordable parking (especially when traveling in an unfamiliar city) can be stressful and a put a strain on your wallet. BestParking will help you avoid parking garage rip-offs by directing you towards the closest and cheapest parking options. In living up to their promise for accuracy, any report of inaccurate pricing is backed up with a $5 Starbucks giftcard. Available for: iOS, Android, and Blackberry

- Expensify: Expensify is designed with easy expense reporting in mind, which makes it ideal for salespeople or traveling business people. Photograph receipts, keep track of miles traveled, and record other travel expenses all on one platform to make your life a little easier. The great part about the receipt photography is that the app is able to read the values on the receipt so no manual entry is necessary. If you're no good at keeping track of your receipts, you can also import credit transactions digitally. Available for: iOS, Android, Windows, and Blackberry

- GameFly: Most gamers have heard of (and used) Gamefly. Earn GameFly rewards and use coupons to save you even more money. The "Game of the Day" app is particularly nice feature that highlights a free or discounted game every single day. Available for: iOS and Android
- Onavo Extend: Are you hit with data overage charges month after month? Onavo Extend allows you to not only keep track of your data expenditure through monthly reports but actually compresses your data and extends your plan! According to the website, you can save up to 80% on your data usage. Not bad for a free app! Available for: iOS and Android
- Appsfire: Hate paying for apps? Appsfire offers free and highly discounted apps every single day. By filling in a little bit of information, the app can make you a list of recommended downloads to suit your interests. Additionally, you can set up a wish list with notifications for deals or discounts on the apps you want to purchase. You can also avoid unimpressive apps by scrolling through ratings and get a heads up on "the next big thing" by browsing through trending applications. Available for: iOS and Android
- BillGuard: Protect yourself against "grey charges," such as hidden fees, billing errors, free-to-paid charges, scams and credit card fraud. Verify and flag charges to your accounts directly through the app. BillGuard will also alert you when a user has flagged a charge similar to one in your account. The app also functions as a dashboard where you can track your spending patterns. Available for: Web and iOS. Price: Free. Premium service costs $4.99/month.
- SavedPlus: Save money every time you spend. Connect your accounts to SavedPlus and select the percentage of every purchase you'd like to save. Every time you buy something, a dollar value will be transferred to your savings account. So for example, if you set your savings percentage to 10% and you make a $75 purchase, $7.50 will transfer from your checking account to your savings account. Available for: Web, iOS and Android. Price: Free.
- Guide Financial: Every week, Guide Financial scans your transactions and sends you a report on your expenditures. You will also receive personalized financial advice and

coupons and deals based on your spending patterns. Available for: Web. Price: Free.

- RedLaser: RedLaser is a barcode-scanning app for price comparisons. Scan a product to find out what it costs at nearby retailers; you can also buy items directly from the app and pick them up in-store. Available for: iOS, Android and Windows Phone. Price: Free.

- ShopSavvy: This barcode and QR scanner shows you product details and price comparisons so you can decide whether to buy in-store or online. Create lists of items you might want to buy later and set price alerts to find when a product has been marked down. Available for: iOS, Android and Windows Phone. Price: Free.

- Price Check by Amazon: Online retail behemoth Amazon has its own barcode scanning app that compares in-store pricing with the prices offered on Amazon.com, plus product descriptions and customer reviews. Available for: iOS and Android. Price: Free.

- RepairPal: RepairPal eliminates the guesswork of finding a good mechanic. Tell them your car's make and model, and it'll give you a repair estimate and recommend "Top Shops" in your area. Available for: Web, iOS and Android. Price: Free.

- Key Ring: Store all of your loyalty cards on your mobile device and enroll in new loyalty programs directly through the app. You'll also receive coupons exclusive to Key Ring. Available for: iOS and Android. Price: Free.

- CardStar: Another way to consolidate your loyalty cards in one app, CardStar also gives you access to daily deals, sales, special offers and coupons from your favorite retailers. Available for: iOS and Android. Price: Free.

- mySuperList: This app is incredible. Whether you do you food shopping online or in store it allows you to make a saving. You can create your shopping list while out and about and then check which supermarket is selling all of those items for the cheapest price. You can also get cashback on certain items with the app meaning even bigger savings. It's a no brainer really. Available for: iPhone Price: Free.

- Idealo: Do you hate buying something on a shopping trip only to find you could have bought it cheaper elsewhere? Idealo is a life saver for anyone who is caught out by making impulse purchases. Just scan the products barcode or enter the keywords to find how much you could get it for from retailers. You can download it here. Great bargaining tool! Available for: iPhone Price: Free.

- Spendometer : The Spendometer is a great budgeting tool and one of the best money saving apps. If you have a smart phone then you need this app in your life. You can set your daily/weekly/monthly budget for a number of items and then fill in your spending as you go along. The spendmeter will tell you how much you are overspending or even saving. Available for: iPhone, Android Price: Free.

- Fashionably Skint: Fashionably Skint gives girls a new and fun way to borrow and lend clothes with friends on campus. The main feature of the app is that it lets you upload photos of clothes that you are willing to share and search for outfits that you may want to borrow from someone nearby (saving you a fortune). Available for: iPhone, Android Price: Free.

Saving:

125 Ways to Save Money

1. Switch your bank accounts to a bank that respects you. Earn some serious interest on your checking and savings accounts. Interest rates are not what they once were, but some of the best free checking accounts and best savings accounts can be found online.

2. Sign up for every free customer rewards program you can. Even if you rarely shop at that place, having a rewards card for that place will eventually net you some coupons and discounts. Create a free email account just for these mailings, collect every card you can, and then check that account for extra coupons whenever you're ready to shop.

3. Use Rewards Credit Cards that give points on purchases at a wide range of stores.

4. Instead of throwing out some damaged clothing repair it instead. Simple sewing can be done by anyone – it just takes a few minutes and it saves a lot of money by keeping you from buying new clothes when you don't really need to.

5. Call your credit card company and ask for a rate reduction. Take any of your credit cards that are carrying a balance, and call the number on the back. Tell them that you want an interest rate reduction or you'll take your business elsewhere. If the first person you talk to won't do it, ask to talk to a supervisor. On a $5,000 balance, even a 3% rate reduction saves you $150 a year.

6. Make a quadruple batch of dinner. Casseroles are nice, easy dishes to prepare, but on busy nights, it's often still easier to just order some take-out which can cost a family of four almost $40. Instead, the next time you make a casserole, make four batches of it and put the other three in the freezer. Next time you need a quick meal for the family, grab one of those batches and just heat it. This idea also allows you to buy the

ingredients in bulk, making each casserole cheaper than it would be ordinarily and also cheaper than trying a prepackaged meal.

7. Be diligent about turning off lights before you leave. If you spend one minute turning off lights before a two hour trip, that's the equivalent of earning $50 an hour. That's some impressive savings, particularly if you do it before longer trips.

8. Install CFL (or, even better, LED) bulbs wherever it makes sense. These bulbs might cost more initially, but they both have a longer life than normal incandescent bulbs and they both eat far less electricity. CFLs tend to use about 25% of the electricity of an incandescent – LEDs use about 2%. CFLs are cheaper than LEDs right now and produce better light, but not quite as good as incandescent bulbs.

9. Install a programmable thermostat. These devices regulate the temperature in your house automatically according to the schedule that you set. Thus, when you're not home, it allows the heating or cooling to turn off for several hours, saving you on your energy bill. A programmable thermostat can easily cut your energy bill by 10 to 20%..

10. Clean your car's air filter. A clean air filter can improve your gas mileage by up to 7%, saving you more than $100 for every 10,000 miles you drive in an average vehicle.

11. Talk to your loved ones about what your dreams are. This seems like an odd way to save money, but if you spend time with the people you care about the most and come to some consensus about your dreams, it becomes easy for you all to plan for it. If you're all planning and working together towards this dream, it becomes easier to stay focused on it and reach it.

12. Do a "maintenance run" on your appliances.. Do some basic home and auto maintenance on a regular schedule. Instead of just waiting until something breaks to deal with it, develop a monthly maintenance schedule where you go around your home (and your car) and perform a bit of maintenance where it's needed. Check them to make sure there isn't any dust

clogging them and that they're fairly clean. Look behind the appliances, and use your vacuum to gently clear away dust. Check all of the vents, especially on refrigerators, dryers, and heating and cooling units. The less dust you have blocking the mechanics of these devices, the more efficiently they'll run (saving you on your energy bill) and the longer they'll last (saving you on replacement costs)This little activity, taking you just an hour or two a month, will keep things from breaking down and help you see problems before they become disasters.

13. Cancel unused club memberships. Are you paying dues at a club that you never use? Like, for instance, a gym membership or a country club membership? Get fit for free! Walk, ride bikes, check out my Pinterest Board of at home workouts or try exercise dvd's. Average savings – at least $40 a month and $480 a year.

14. Wash your hands regularly. Just by washing your hands thoroughly each time you use the bathroom or handle raw foods, you'll keep yourself from acquiring all kinds of viruses and bacteria, saving you on medical bills and medicine costs and lost productivity.

15. Switch to term life insurance. Despite what your insurance sales person says, insurance is not necessarily an investment especially if you need to get yourself out of debt and start building some wealth. Universal and whole policies are much more expensive and offer a sub-par investment opportunity. Every situation is different, and your health or risk tolerance are to be considered.

16. Go for reliability and fuel efficiency when buying a car. A reliable and fuel efficient car will save you thousands over the long haul. If you drive a vehicle for 80,000 miles, and you choose a 25 miles per gallon car over a 15 miles per gallon car, you save 2,133 gallons of gas. At $3 a gallon, that's $6,400 in savings. A friend of mine has an electric car (that has a gas take back up) which gives them 150mpg. Yes! That is not a typo. Their annual gas bill when gas prices were reaching $4/gallon was only $100 per year. Reliability can pay the same in money for repairs saved.

17. Rent out unused space in your home. Do you have an extra bedroom that's not being used?
18. Get rid of unread magazine subscriptions.
19. Find or create a babysitting co-op. Each family takes a turn watching the kids each month or each quarter. Swap babysitting with neighbors. There are a lot of parents out there who are quite willing to swap babysitting nights, saving you (and them) the money of hiring one for an evening out.
20. Invest in a deep freezer. A deep freezer, after the initial investment, is a great bargain. You can use it to store all sorts of bulk foods, which enables you to pay less per pound of it at the market. You can store lots of meals prepared in advance, enabling you to just go home and pop something homemade (and cheap) in the oven.
21. Look for a cheaper place to live. Take a serious look about moving to a less expensive area – if you can find work there, then a move can definitely put you in better financial shape.
22. Take public transportation. If the city's transit system is available near you, take it to work (or to play) instead of driving your car. It's far cheaper and you don't have to worry about parking your vehicle.
23. Carpool. Is there anyone that lives near you who works at the same place (or near the same place) that you do? Why not ride together, alternating drivers each day? You can halve the wear and tear and gas costs for your car – and for your acquaintance as well.
24. Design your "debt snowball. Everyone needs a plan to help them get out of debt, so sit down and plot out what debts you're going to pay off and in what order. Simply having a plan goes a long way towards bringing that plan into action, and paying off debts early is one of the surest ways to put money in your pocket over the long run.
25. Go through your cell phone bill, look for services you don't use, and eliminate them.
26. Comparison shop other cell providers. A friend of mine pays $300 for cell services for four phones. I pay $100 for four phones. That's a savings of $2400 a year.

27. Consolidate your student loans. Interest rates are quite low right now, so it might be worthwhile to consolidate your student loans into one low-rate package. Look into the various student loan consolidation packages – even a 1% reduction on a $10,000 loan saves you $100 a year – and your loan is probably bigger than that (and the rate cut you could get is probably bigger).

28. Get on an automatic debt repayment plan for any student loans you have. Some student loans offer a rate reduction if you sign up for their automatic debt repayment plan. Some claim savings of about $60 a year.

29. When buying a car, go for late model used. These are typically cars coming straight off of leases, meaning they were cared for by reliable owners.

30. Find out about all of the benefits of your job. Most people aren't even aware of all of the benefits available to them. Spend some time with an HR person finding out about all the benefits of your job – you might be surprised at what you might find. Free tickets to sporting events, free personal improvement opportunities, and an optional employee match on some retirement funds that maximized the money are some examples of what you could find.

31. Don't speed. Not only is it inefficient in terms of gasoline usage, it also can get you pulled over and cost you a bundle, as I discovered a while back. It's highly cost-efficient to just drive the speed limit, keep that gas in the tank, and keep the cops off your tail.

32. Buy a smaller house. You don't need a giant place to live. Instead, buy something more modest and you'll find yourself with plenty of room – and still plenty of cash in your pocket from a smaller mortgage, lower property taxes, and lower utility costs.

33. Drive a different route to work if you find yourself "automatically" stopping for something on the way into work or the way home. This is a powerful tip for those who overspend on groceries or coffee stops. Get rid of that constant drain by selecting a different route that doesn't go by the temptation, even if the new route is a bit longer.

34. Air seal your home. Most homes have some air leaks that make the job of keeping it cool in summer and warm in winter that much harder – and that much more costly for you. Spend an afternoon air sealing your home – the DoE has a great guide on basic airsealing.

35. Unplug – Phantom Electricity is the electricity that is used when a device is plugged in but not in use. For example…you leave your cell phone charger plugged in all the time, but you only charge your phone every few days…did you know that your charger is still using electricity when it is plugged in but not charging? This is "Phantom Electricity", and little bits are being used throughout your home every day. Make sure all your electrical devices are on a surge protector. This is especially true of your entertainment center and your computer equipment. A power surge can damage these electronics very easily, so spend the money for a basic surge protector and keep your equipment plugged into such a device. Upgrade that surge protector to a smart strip, and you can also save my turning the surge off and thus closing off the continual power that flows even to plugged in devices that are turned off.

36. Cancel the cable or satellite channels you don't watch. Many people with cable services often are paying for a premium package but rarely watch those extra channels. Get rid of the excess channels and put that cash back in your pocket.

37. Don't let the mistakes of your past drag you down into more mistakes. Look ahead to the future. The choices you make now won't affect the past – but they definitely will affect the future. Think back, and remember how the bad choices you made earlier are costing you now, and constantly remember to not make those mistakes now so that they don't cost your future.

38. Never give up. Whenever the struggle against debt feels like it's too much, go read a personal finance blog and remember that there are a lot of people out there fighting the same fight. Read around through the archives and learn some new things – and perhaps

get inspired to keep going, no matter what. Talk to your Women's Money Mentor for support as well.

39. Change your attitude to your mortgage. If you can afford to make overpayments on your mortgage, you'll clear your debt several years early and make massive savings. For example, if you borrow $100,000 at 6% over 25 years, you'll pay it back at $643 a month. The total charge for credit will be $93,000. But if you can overpay by $100 a month you'll clear the loan in less than 19 years, giving you 6 years of mortgage-free living and saving a staggering $25,000 in interest.

40. Clear your credit card debt. One of the golden rules of financial planning is to clear your most expensive debts first, in other words your credit cards. OK, credit cards offer a convenient way to pay for goods and services but if you can't clear the balance every month, consider a low-cost loan as an alternative or create a 0 interest balance transfer system to pay your credit card debt faster with no interest. This takes a good amount of planning if you cannot pay off your debt in the 0% interest amount of time because you will have to apply for another card with 0% balance transfer in 12-18 months, so plan ahead and keep your credit score up.

41. Consider installing a tankless water heater. Electric Tankless Water Heaters, also called Instantaneous On Demand Water Heaters, provide endless hot water on demand and only as needed. Self-modulating flow sensor technology regulates the amount of energy required to heat the water needed. They can be 99.8-percent energy efficient. You can save up to 60-percent on your water heating cost.

42. Consider a pay-as-you go mobile. If you've ever argued that that a mobile phone is a necessity rather than a luxury – great news, you win! If you hand over $50 a month to your mobile phone company, that's $600 a year. You can buy phones for less than $30 and purchase pay- as-you-go vouchers for not much more. Do the math. If you save money, make the switch.

43. Know what you owe. To get where you need to be, you need to know where you are starting. Gather up all your statements and determine how much you owe in

total. If you don't like the answer, this negative exercise can give you the oomph to get going.

44. Having a spending plan for your income is the best way to ensure that you are spending your hard-earned money in the way you want and most importantly, in the way that assures your financial success.

45. Review your income tax withholding. If you are receiving a tax refund of more than $600, you are providing an interest-free loan to the IRS. A better idea is to adjust your withholding -- have less money taken out for income taxes -- and use those funds earning zero percent interest to help pay down your high interest consumer debt.

46. Start an automatic savings plan. The simplest way to avoid unwanted debt is to have money set aside for those unexpected or large expenses that we all have. When you have money taken from your paycheck or checking account and automatically deposited into a savings account, you will hardly notice. But you will be building a very important financial tool -- liquid savings. Your savings goal should be six months to a year of living expenses.

47. Half of nothing is actually something. Commit money you don't have yet to paying down your debt. Use at least 50 percent of any new raises, bonuses, tax refunds or other source of additional income to give yourself a boost in paying off expensive debt or towards emergency savings.

48. Set up automatic electronic banking payments. A late payment can trigger a hefty late fee, and may result in an increased interest rate on future credit card purchases. Electronic payments will help avoid a payment arriving late and increasing the cost of your debt.

49. Keep your score high. Take some time to review your credit reports to make sure they contain accurate information. Get a copy of your reports for free at AnnualCreditReport.com. If you have ugly credit caused by errors, this will hurt your credit score. If you find inaccurate information, dispute the item with the credit bureau that reported it. Poor credit costs you thousands of extra dollars in higher interest payments.

Reportedly people with good credit save tens of thousands of dollars on car payments, mortgages,and credit card debt. Check your score at creditkarma.com or credit.com for free.

50. Don't fall for debt settlement scams or schemes. Lenders don't want to settle. If you must, use an attorney or don't do it at all.

51. Don't pay for student loan consolidation. The government offers that as a free service.

52. Don't forget to plan for 2010 holiday expenses. Every year, people seek help after the holidays because overspending on gifts, travel and other holiday expenses pushes them over the financial edge. Set a limit, fund it with yearlong savings and enjoy the season for a change.

53. Ignoring a financial problem will only make matters worse. Get professional help now if you need it. You can find a trusted, nonprofit, free credit counseling agency at Aiccca.org or Nfcc.org. Card issuers are now required to include a toll-free number for credit counseling on statements.

54. Each week, call a new company that you deal with (insurance, cable, phone) and ask if they will lower your rate.

55. Keep track of what food is routinely getting thrown out, and buy less of it or not at all.

56. Ditch your cable and satellite service for services like Netflix, Amazon Prime and Hulu. Look into those or at least cut back on premium channels and services. Go a step further and ditch services such as Netflix, Amazon Prime and Hulu to viewing only free online streaming from Hulu, CBS, and NBC.

57. See if your community has a produce auction and learn to preserve items that can be purchased in bulk for much cheaper.

58. Kids can ride the school bus, they don't have to be driven.

59. Line dry what you can.

60. Get a blanket for the hot water heater. Turn it down a degree or two.

61. Get foam pipe insulation if your pipes are in an unheated basement.

62. Put in little insulators behind switch plates and find any other drafty areas.
63. Not all clothing needs to be laundered after one wearing. Spruce up with misting and re-ironing when
64. See if you can get your hair done at the local vo-tech school. They also sometimes do oil changes, wash dogs and have inexpensive restaurants.
65. Donate what you are not using and get the tax deduction.
66. Many of us overdo it at the holidays. Stop. Make a budget and stick to it, whether it be Christmas, Easter or a child's birthday.
67. With the money you are saving, save enough so that when some bills come you can take advantage of things like "pay in full now and save 10%."
68. For one month, record every penny that is spent in your household. What can be eliminated?
69. Are you still paying PMI? Do you need to be?
70. Can you refinance your home to a lower interest rate?
71. Do a weekly meal plan and then grocery list, and stick to it. That link will also show you how to do a method of meal planning that saves money.
72. Look at your pantry and freezer. Overfull and nothing to eat? Every quarter try to empty your pantry. Can you go an entire month without purchasing groceries if you just put a little more effort in creative meal planning and cooking? If you can, playing this game of "Pantry on Parade" can lead to an average savings of $500.
73. Cut things in half. Water down cleansers and detergents. Cut dryer sheets in half. Use less. Don't always grab two tissues or two paper towels if you only need one.
74. Make sure you learn how to use all of your appliances effectively–what is the best setting on your dishwasher, washer, dryer, refrigerator for optimum running?
75. Use only cold water for washing clothes.
76. Are you paying for a storage unit to hold your stuff? Sell your stuff, leave your storage unit days behind (vowing never to repeat), and save the money from the unit. The average spend on a storage unit is $80 a month. That's $960 a year.
77. Is your garage full of unwanted or unused stuff? Sell your stuff, clean out the garage and put your car in the

garage. The average spend on car washes is $20 a month. That's $240 a year.

78. If you travel for business, see if you can add on extra days for personal vacation with your family. You could possibly trim the travel costs of one whole family member.

79. If you live in an area with utility choices, shop around and compare rates.

80. Learn how to use common household items like vinegar, baking soda and lemons around the house and for cleaning. Vinegar and water is much cheaper than many household cleaners!

81. Before committing to an expensive Costco or similar warehouse club membership, try it out and make sure it is less money. It often isn't. Look online and see if they have "try it free" offers for 30 or 60 days.

82. See if your veterinarian has special months when they run discounted vaccinations or teeth cleaning.

83. If you are good about using credit cards and pay them off, consider putting all of your monthly expenses on one that will get you some type of rewards—either cash back or gift cards. Make sure that the benefits outweigh any fees.

84. Overcome the awkwardness…and approach family members about setting spending limits when it comes to gift giving.

85. Use the Box Tops for Education program or the Giant program or some other way to donate money to schools instead of actual money.

86. Unless your situation is complex, use one of the $40-$50 or free tax preparation programs like TaxAct instead of paying someone to do it.

87. Look at your local banks and credit unions. They generally offer more personable service and better savings interest rate return on your money, definitely Years ago a local bank which at a time when big banks were offering .01% interest on savings (with withdrawal penalties), was offering 1.61% on a checking account! It's lower now, but still way higher than any other offerings.

88. Almost everything goes on the credit card, which is payed off in full every month so no fees are tacked on. This

not only gets an excellent credit history, but gets you cash back in rewards every so often, so I actually make money off using the card.

89. Freeze meat on sale. Buy a LOT of it; then cut sirloin roasts into steaks or stir-fry strips or divide it up otherwise into half-pound portions (2x1/4 lb portions) and freeze tons of it in zippered sandwich bags. (Adding marinade to chicken or beef helps avoid freezer burn).

90. Some banks have programs that automatically transfer $1 for each debit transaction made including online bills from your checking to your savings account. Over a year's time that can add up to over $1,600!

91. Some banks offer to "round up" all your debit card transactions to the nearest dollar -, if your purchase is $3.26 they would charge $4.00 and transfer the difference to your savings.

92. Try the 52 Week Money Challenge. The first week of the year, you put $1 in a jar. The following week, $2, and so forth and so on. (There are spreadsheets online that have it all mapped out.) At the end of the year, you'll have a little over $1300 saved! Try Carrie Rocha's advice in this chapter for a new and effective twist to the 52 week challenge.

93. Saving money should have been first. Everyone on any income can save a little bit of money a month. Even if it is change you find or have left over from cash purchases. Start somewhere…anywhere. Saving money starts as a mindset, and has little to do with the actual amount saved…that part ends up growing with time.

94. Have a balance range of approximately 2 months of bills in your checking account. Any time the balance goes over the top end of the amount, put the money into savings.

95. Look first for small savings - not because they'll end your budget problems, but simply because they're easy to find and take advantage of. For example, swear off that mid-afternoon, expensive premium latte. Shop for clothes and household furnishings only during sales. Higher gasoline prices make it a good idea to "bundle" shopping trips. Keep your house warmer in summer

and cooler in winter. Take on chores that you usually pay someone else to perform, such as mowing the lawn or shoveling snow. Seemingly inconsequential savings do, in fact, add up.

96. Cut your taxes. Usually this means taking better advantage of itemized deductions, which is a lot easier to do if you're either self-employed or have some income from work you do outside of a regular job. That opens up a range of new deductions - from expenses for work-related items to a home office - that are much harder to claim if you're an ordinary working stiff.

97. On the investment side, you can save some money by selling, and then writing off, investments that have lost money. You can use such losses to offset any gains you may have in a given year. If your losses outweigh your gains, you can deduct as much as $3,000 of investment losses from your ordinary income each year. Those with higher incomes may also be able to save some money by shifting money out of taxable bonds into tax-free municipal bonds.

98. Appeal your home assessment. If you're a homeowner, you may even be able to cut your real estate taxes by challenging the value that the local assessor puts on your property. You have to have good evidence, of course. You should call the assessor's office first to make sure you understand the formula for determining the house's value (the assessment listed on tax bills is often only a fraction of the real value that determines your tax). If recent home sales in your neighborhood lead you to believe that your house is worth less than its assessment and a qualified real estate agent writes an appraisal in support of your claim, then you can file a grievance with the assessor's office and possibly get your bill reduced. The cost: $200 to $300 for the written appraisal. If an attorney handles the appeal for you, he or she will typically charge 50% of the first year's tax savings.

99. Make a family game out of saving money. The goal is to try to cut your spending by $400 a month. Did you know if you cut your spending by $13 a day, you'll save $400 a month? That is $4800 a year (which can be the price of two years of community college)!

100. Call your utility companies to make sure you're getting the best rate, and to make sure you really need all the services you're paying for like call waiting or premium cable channels. A few phone calls usually yields savings of $15 a month. If you live in a deregulated state, make sure you're shopping around for the best electricity rate! It's easy! In Texas, go to PowerToChoose.org, enter your zip code, see rates, read the fine print and choose a provider. The process is similar for all deregulated states, and there's no interruption to your service. Also check with your electric company about flex rates, that is, electricity is generally cheaper late at night or during the work day, and some companies will re-rate accordingly. If you can run the dishwasher after 10 p.m. or do all your computer stuff at a certain time, you can cut money off your bill (but you may have to sign up specifically for that program).

101. Shop around and compare rates on auto and home insurance. Ask yourself if you could live with a higher deductible or different limits, and make sure you are taking advantage of all the discounts available to you (security system, good student, student away).

102. If you've had a disruption to your cable or satellite service, call and ask for a refund! Legitimate complaints may also result in a credit on your cell phone bill.

103. The Return of the Clothesline – Start using a clothesline or drying rack, and you'll save nearly 6% on your monthly electric bill according to the Department of Energy…plus your house will be quieter & cooler! If your city or homeowners association prohibits clotheslines, your best option is a cloths drying rack (available at Target, Walmart and Bed Bath & Beyond for about $30). If your monthly electric bill is $200, your clothesline just saved you about $12 a month - $144 a year!

104. Find a Farmer's Market – Discover your local farmer's market, and your budget will love the prices and you'll love the fresh taste of just picked produce! To find a farmer's market near you, visit LocalHarvest.org or BountifulBaskets.org.

105. Reusable Lunch Containers – Instead of a brown bag, carry a lunch box. Instead of zip top bags, invest in reusable bags. You'll spend a little money upfront, but you'll save money in the long run.

106. Homemade Cleaning Products – Make the switch to homemade cleaning products that cost pennies to make and clean just as well without harsh chemicals.

107. Repurpose – Look twice at things before throwing them away! Could you cut off the fronts of some of your Christmas cards to use a gift tags next year? Could you paint that old piece of furniture or spray paint a chandelier to give it a new life?

108. Are you taking advantage of your flex plan at work for pre-tax savings?

109. Ask your doctor about any money saving prescription options…the last time I did this, I was given samples each time. My prescription was $575 a month with no generic option! Samples saved me over $12,000 in prescriptions. Ask and you just might receive!

110. Can your doctor prescribe a cheaper alternative? Save money on prescriptions by avoiding "combo pills." A combo pill combines more than one type of medication. For example, Lotrel is a blood pressure medicine that costs $70 a month for generic, but you could get a prescription for the two components (Amlodipine and Benazepril) for $6 each. Ask your doctor.

111. No dental insurance? Find a dental school in your area for exams.

112. Check out FREE diet websites like SparkPeople.com and MyFitnessPal.com. Simply input your weight, your desired weight, and you'll get a plan. These sites help you keep a food diary and keep count of calories, fat, protein and carbs. This can improve your health which improves your medical expenses. In addition, you may find a decrease in your grocery expenses.

113. Travel Tip: Find the deal first, destination second – this is The Budget Diet's motto when it comes to saving on travel. It simply means don't get your heart set on a destination, and then discover the deals don't exist. Instead, be open-minded about a destination and get excited about great deals.

114. Did you know that discounted gift cards exist for travel? Costco has been known to offer $300 American Airlines gift cards for $269.99. There is huge selection of discounted gift cards at CardCash.com and Giftcards.com you'll find discounted gift cards for hotels, restaurants, shopping and more!

115. Save on Cruises with VacationsToGo.com's 90-day last minute ticker. It's not unusual to find discounts of 75%!

116. Consider a home exchange program like HomeExchange.com or AffordableTravelClub.com

117. Don't assume a road trip is always budget friendly! Calculate the miles and gas used/cost. You may find it's cheaper to fly via a low-cost carrier like Allegiant, Spirit, or even Southwest airlines.

118. Don't assume cheap flights that charge for baggage are cheaper than airlines that include baggage. If your dates are flexible, you may be able to fly for $10 more, but your bags fly free…saving you $60.

119. Can you make it yourself or fix it yourself? Thanks to You Tube, there's a video to teach you just about anything! You can even learn to fix a leaky toilet!

120. Cut and color your hair, and do mani-pedis at home.

121. Hyper- mile- ing. Hypermileing. Slow acceleration saves a ton of gas, as well as letting the weight of your car take you to red lights, etc. My van has a miles per gallon currently setting. I tried this and watched it go from 11.5 to 13.7 miles to the gallon. I have learned how to get an extra 2.2 miles to the gallon when I drive that thing. I usually drive my more effective car but to watch it, I tested this in the van with a meter to watch my savings. I apply this in all my cars. I have heard that you can Google search hypermileing on Google and find out more. (I must add I live in a FLAT part of the country)

122. Treat Your Self: Make a list of small inexpensive things you can splurge on. Something out of the ordinary to look forward to. Set a small price limit, allot for it and choose one each week or two. It's like a little pat on the back for keeping up with your budget. If you just keep denying yourself over and over you will get worn down and not likely stick to the constraints you've made.

123. Online Savings Accounts: They have a higher annual percentage yield. So if you have a larger sum of money that you have just been keeping in your bank's savings than you might as well make more on it. You can transfer it between your accounts so it is still available to you. Ally or CapitalOne 360 (formerly ING) are two popular online accounts.

124. Split purchasing club memberships, like Costco or Sam's Club, with a friend. You might also decide to shop together and split the purchases getting half the amount at the bulk price.

125. Scout out hidden fees. The charges attached to mutual funds can really take a bite out of your holdings. If a fund's expense ratio is 1.5% may sound small, but that's $15 per $1000 invested…for every year of your investment!! If you have a return of 8%, that's $80…almost 20% of your gain is paid to fees, and if your gain goes down, you still pay the fees. Most funds sold by brokers also have a broker fee attached that gets charged when you buy or sell. You can find actively managed funds with .5% or 1%, and index funds with .19%.

Visit us at WomensMoney.org for free online tools and more.

www.womensmoney.org